D0422358

RESEARCH IN INDUSTRIAL HUMAN RELATIONS

INDUSTRIAL RELATIONS RESEARCH ASSOCIATION

•

PUBLICATION NO. 17

•

(The previous books in this series were published by the Association, in Madison, Wisconsin, with the exception of No. 11, MANPOWER IN THE UNITED STATES, and No. 15, EMERGENCY DISPUTES AND NATIONAL POLICY, both published by Harper & Brothers, New York.)

RESEARCH IN INDUSTRIAL HUMAN RELATIONS

A CRITICAL APPRAISAL

EDITORIAL BOARD

Conrad M. Arensberg
Columbia University

Solomon Barkin
Textile Workers Union of America

W. Ellison Chalmers
University of Illinois

Harold L. Wilensky
University of Michigan

James C. Worthy
Sears, Roebuck and Company

Barbara D. Dennis
Technical Editor
University of Illinois

HARPER & BROTHERS PUBLISHERS
NEW YORK

RESEARCH IN INDUSTRIAL HUMAN RELATIONS

Printed in the United States of America

FIRST EDITION

M-F

Library of Congress catalog card number: 56-9087

CONTENTS

PART IV

TRADE UNIONS

PREFACE

The people of every society, primitive or modern, must face the problem of organizing their work—they must decide what is to be done and how and who is going to do it for what rewards. They must train and motivate people to carry out the tasks they consider important.

Labor economists have long dealt with one aspect of the organization of work in the society at large—the allocation of human productive resources among the various types of productive activity of an economy. They have dealt with how work is organized and wages are set in different kinds of labor markets—what determines where people will work, at what jobs, and at what wages.

This volume is also concerned with the organization of work, and it deals with organizations which have economic purposes. But it emphasizes the noneconomic aspects of the organization of work, the human relations aspects.

"Human relations in industry" has become both the label of a group of studies of people at work and the slogan of a movement of thought and action in American industrial relations. Human relations research and its applications in industry have aroused much heated controversy. The critics of the "human relations approach" have charged that in its preoccupation with improving face-to-face relations at the work station level it (1) underplays conflicts of interest and ideology between employers, workers, and union leaders and therefore misses the central character of industrial relations; and (2) is blind to crucial outside determinants of human relations in the work group—e.g., to the organizational structure of the enterprise, and to the social, political, and economic setting within which human relations arise and have meaning. The critics charge further that this underplaying of interest conflicts and this blindness to the industrial environment lead to a mistaken assumption of a harmony of interests, a management bias, a narrow view of the origins and functions of unions, and exclusive attention to management's problem of maintaining authority and efficiency. Labor critics especially have accented the last point. They claim that much human relations research seems to imply that programs of supervisory training, worker participation, improved communications, and enlightened personnel management would make unions superfluous.

The researchers under attack not only deny the charges, but they have suggested that changes in worker-supervisor-manager-union leader relations at every level have in given cases resulted in increased harmony and efficiency, stronger not weaker unions, or at least more benefit to workers, and that if the "environment" is so important in shaping workplace behavior and collective bargaining relations it is up to the critics to demonstrate the specific corrections.

This volume aims to take a fresh look at these controversies. The editors asked specialists from different disciplines representing many points of view to appraise the research and shed light on the controversies. At the outset we assumed that it would be more useful to ask, "What do we know about the behavior of people at work and the circumstances that gave rise to management's interest in human relations?" than to reiterate the charges and denials of "management bias" in the research. We also assumed that critical and selective reporting of illustrative findings would be more useful than an extensive survey of what has become a vast and varied literature.[1]

Part I accordingly offers two interpretations of the emergence of scholarly and managerial interest in human relations in the workplace, and two appraisals of the uses and limits of social research in industry. The effort is to put the human relations movement in historical perspective and discuss the relation between social scientist and practitioner, and at the same time sample the findings of current research.

Part II focuses on the interplay between what goes on in the urban-industrial environment, on the one hand, and what goes on in the workplace, on the other. Chapter IV gives an overview of some dramatic changes in the technological, social, and cultural environment of people at work. In a decade that seems likely to produce a 35-hour week, it seems appropriate to consider the relation between work and leisure, the theme of Chapter V. Chapter VI

[1] A bibliography of many such surveys, as well as several references to articles dealing with the problem of values in social research are cited in Chapter III.

gives special attention to those features of the economic environment that can help us understand work behavior and the collective bargaining relations that grow out of the problems of work.

People at work are found in organizations and groups, and Parts III and IV offer analyses of two types of organizations: industrial and union.

Organizations vary as to size, criteria for membership, provision for selection of leaders, control structure, degree of centralization, scope of interests, degree of conflict with the external environment, etc. But whatever the variations, one thing is sure: authority gets exercised in all of them. Much of the controversy over human relations research and its applications centers around the question of the facts and the sources of authority and how it is used (e.g., is management using the tools of social science to "manipulate" its workers, etc.). Chapter VII discusses the nature of authority and the commentary which follows discusses its uses in industry from a union point of view. Chapter VIII spells out some differences and similarities between large-scale management and union organizations, giving both caution and encouragement to those who like to see matching tendencies in the internal life of both. Compare Chapter XIII.

While work goes on in organizations, the immediate experience of the participant takes place in small work groups. Chapter IX discusses research on the internal dynamics of these work groups and their functions in the large formal organizations in which they are embedded. Chapter X describes and evaluates different procedures used to change human relations in work groups—e.g., training programs—and reports research aimed to create and study organizational change.

The trade union has been viewed as an integral part of the "social system of the factory," important mainly as it affects management decisions and organizations. Chapter XI spells out this union impact. The union has also been viewed in its own right as a large-scale administrative organ with its own problems of leadership, succession, communication, control, morale, etc. Chapter XIII provides an analysis of human relations in the union. That collective bargaining is affected by economic and other aspects of the environment is suggested by Chapters III and VI. Chapter XII, however, offers the view that much collective bargaining behavior can be explained in psychological terms, whatever the structure of the relationship.

This volume is intended to provide some perspectives for an evaluation of human relations studies and practices. The thirteen authors do not represent one point of view, and their statements are neither definitive nor noncontroversial. One of the purposes of the editors was to bring together within a single volume some of the more important of the conflicting points of view. Men of action in industry and unions, like men in academic settings, can appreciate the necessity of competition in ideas in arriving at the truth. They know, too, that today's truth is always tentative. It is in this spirit that all the authors and the editors have written.

CONRAD M. ARENSBERG
SOLOMON BARKIN
W. ELLISON CHALMERS
HAROLD L. WILENSKY
JAMES C. WORTHY

PART I

SCHOLARS AND PRACTITIONERS: THE HUMAN RELATIONS MOVEMENT

· I ·

MANAGERS, WORKERS, AND IDEAS IN THE UNITED STATES*

BY REINHARD BENDIX
University of California

The purpose of this essay is to trace briefly the major ideological themes concerning the relations between employers and workers which make up the history of American business thinking during the last half century.

THE STRUGGLE FOR SURVIVAL AND THE POWER OF THOUGHT

Fifty years ago economic success was identified with virtue and wealth was regarded as a sign of special merit. "Business is religion, and religion is business," declared the Rev. M. D. Babcock in 1900. "If God gives us the possibilities and the power to get wealth, to acquire influence, to be forces in the world, what is the true conception of life but divine ownership and human administration?"[1] In line with such opinions the captains of industry were hailed as equal to the great men of the past, as leaders of men and nations. They had proved their superior abilities in the relentless struggle for survival. Without their beneficial guidance the masses of the

* This essay is based on Chap. 5 of my book, *Work and Authority in Industry* (New York: Wiley, 1956); documentation is contained in this chapter and only references for direct quotations are cited in the following essay. The book deals with "ideologies of management in the course of industrialization."

[1] Cited in A. W. Griswold, *The American Gospel of Success* (Master's dissertation, Yale University, 1933), p. 89.

people would live in squalor and want. In this view society was divided between employers and their men, between the success of the few who possessed the power to originate and conduct great enterprises and the failure of the many who did not.

Harsh as this doctrine was, it was believed by many who but for the human tolerance of ambiguity stood condemned in their own eyes. For many worshiped at the altar of success, who were not successful themselves. But the doctrine of the survival of the fittest had no place for this large middle-class public which stood midway between the success of the few and the failure of the many. That intellectual vacuum was filled by adding a quasireligious celebration of "mental power" to the standard celebration of the successful tycoon. "Business success is due to certain qualities of mind. Anything is yours if you only want it hard enough. Just think of that. *Anything*. Try it. Try it in earnest and you will succeed. It is the operation of a mighty law."[2]

No one questioned this emphasis, since the "new thought" was a close kin to the "old effort." Many who believed in success but did not attain it, could gather up new courage for the endless quest from these optimistic and comfortably vague admonitions. Similarly, "self-help" had originally referred to the hard work and drive of the individual businessman. But in a market increasingly dominated by large enterprises, this meaning was gradually obscured by a "how-to" literature which identified self-help with a man's ability to do his own repair work around the house. In a society in which success and the successful received unstinted and unremitting praise these were minor themes, to be sure, which merely foreshadowed subsequent changes in the thinking of American employers.

THE IDEOLOGY OF THE OPEN-SHOP

Before the Great Depression most employers saw no reason to embellish the harshness of the struggle for survival. Typically, there were two ways in which the doctrines were applied to the relations between employers and employees. One was intellectually consistent in emphasizing the struggle for existence. A man like William Graham Sumner found the belief in competition clearly inconsist-

[2] Cited in *ibid.*, pp. 101-102.

ent with the idea of cooperation. Employers wanted to have labor plentiful but capital scarce and well rewarded, while workers wanted to have capital plentiful but labor scarce and highly paid. The interests of the two groups were antagonistic, and no two ways about it. Sumner even went so far as to endorse strikes and trade unions; to him these were necessary weapons in the workers' struggle for survival. A strike was justified, Sumner thought, "if the men win the advance. . . . If they did not win, it proves that they were wrong to strike."[3] Such logic made no sense to employers who had to deal with the labor problem first-hand. For them competition stopped at the plant door; inside, they wanted cooperation, and they were not getting it. They read with approval the diatribes of Elbert Hubbard, who commiserated with the "employer who grows old before his time in a vain attempt to get frowzy ne'er-do-wells to do intelligent work."[4] And while for a time they were content to denounce the "help" that does nothing but loaf when the employer's back is turned, they felt forced to take sterner measures when the membership of trade unions increased from 400,000 to 2 million between 1897 and 1904. This rise of trade union activity challenged American employers at the very pinnacle of their social recognition, and it challenged their absolute authority in the management of their enterprises. As is well known, words and violence followed.

It had been a sacrosanct belief that every employer should be free to handle his own labor problem as he saw fit; but now it was admitted (at the NAM convention of 1903) that the challenge of the trade unions justified a departure from this approach. Principles of management were announced where before the autocratic discretion of the employer had been taken for granted—not that these principles did anything but formulate the accepted views, that the authority of management was absolute, that employers and workers were "free" to fire or quit at a moment's notice, that the employee was duty-bound to work peacefully and loyally. But the more or less violent methods of the open-shop campaign, which applied these "principles," had other far-reaching consequences. In

[3] W. G. Sumner, *What Social Classes Owe Each Other* (New York: Harper, 1883), pp. 91-92.

[4] Elbert Hubbard, *A Message to Garcia* (New York: New York Public Library, 1930), p. 14. The book was first published in 1899.

the course of fighting the unions, employers were giving conscious attention to the problems of labor-management. And by insisting upon the compliance of the workers rather than upon their initiative and competitive drive, they were beginning to undermine their own belief in struggle for survival. By what they did rather than by what they said, American employers were questioning Abraham Lincoln's hope for every man "to be a hired labourer this year and the next, work for himself afterwards, and finally hire men to work for him." In the course of the open-shop campaign the employers were saying in effect that it was they who prescribed the conditions which decided upon the worker's success or failure.

SCIENTIFIC MANAGEMENT AND MANAGERIAL IDEOLOGY

The open-shop campaign went hand in hand with the rise of scientific management. If the one asserted the absolute authority of the employers, the other was ready to prescribe what to do with it. By finding the "one best way" of doing each job, scientific management would maximize output and hence the earnings of workers and the profits of employers. Expectations soared on what could be accomplished along these lines. Hugo Muensterberg was sure that the cultural gain would be even greater than the commercial profit. "As soon as every one can be brought to the place where his best energies may be unfolded . . . mental dissatisfaction in the work, mental depression and discouragement may be replaced in our social community by overflowing joy and perfect inner harmony."[5] Wealth and happiness would be the reward of those who took sufficient thought, though the means now proposed were the methods of science rather than "mental power" or "a wealthy attitude of mind."

Scientific management has often been considered as a series of techniques for increasing efficiency in production, such as better cost accounting methods, premium payments, time and motion studies, and so on. Frederick Taylor, the originator of the movement, vigorously protested against this interpretation. These devices, singly or taken together, were not scientific management as he understood it. His main object was "to remove the causes for antag-

[5] Hugo Muensterberg, *Psychology and Industrial Efficiency* (Boston: Houghton, Mifflin, 1913), p. 308.

onism between the boss and the men who were under him."[6] And that object could be attained only by a "mental revolution" on the part of workers and employers. Scientific management had to be adopted willingly by both parties, who must "take their eyes off of the division of the surplus as the all-important matter, and together turn their attention toward increasing the size of the surplus."[7] If they did, the surplus would become so large as to eliminate all friction between them.

But while employers and workers first had to turn their attention toward increasing the surplus, the methods for accomplishing this end were those of scientific management. These methods had important consequences for industrial relations, as Taylor saw it. Once adopted, trade unions would not exist and collective bargaining would be at a minimum—a mere formality. The reason? Workers would be free to present their complaints, individually or collectively. Under scientific management such grievances would not be subject to arbitrary personal judgments; instead they would be the object of scientific investigation. The result should be satisfactory to both sides. Furthermore, the old-fashioned dictatorial methods would be eliminated from industry. For managers as well as workers had to follow to the letter the rules established by scientific management (Taylor's contracts included the statement "The company must do as I tell them.").[8] These rules would be equitable and impartial.

In the past it had been assumed that a worker's inefficiency and low output were his own fault, for which he would have to suffer the consequences. If he did not do better, he would be disciplined or fired. Now Taylor maintained that the prosperity of all would be diminished, if the men did not work at their highest efficiency. Gradually management was assuming greater responsibilities than it had before by assessing each worker's abilities and by improving the methods of job-placement. As "instant dismissal" became a measure of last resort, the task became to keep workers on their jobs and actually to see to it that they did their best. Under these circum-

[6] Frederick W. Taylor, *Scientific Management* (New York: Harper, 1947), pp. 128-129.

[7] *Ibid.*, pp. 29-30.

[8] Cited in F. B. Copley, *Frederick W. Taylor* (New York: Harper, 1923), I, p. 417.

stances hard work and compliance counted for more than initiative and competitive drive.

By the 1920's there were signs that the image of the worker was changing. From a man whose laziness was denounced or whose diligence was praised, he became a man whose abilities had to be tested and improved by training. No doubt, American employers would have been indignant at the suggestion that they were about to abandon the American dream. But the fact remains that during the 1920's the old formulas were beginning to lose their magic certainty. What would be put in their place?

CHANGING IMAGES OF MAN IN INDUSTRY

American employers were clearly confronted with an unprecedented situation. In the past they had only reiterated the received opinions which helped to explain and justify their economic self-interest. But when Taylor proposed that management put the selection and training of workers on a scientific basis, he involved industrialists in intellectual debates for which their training and interests had not prepared them.

Increasingly the employers proposed to do something about the defects of character which they deplored in their workers. But, along with their efforts to provide more effective incentives, speculation increased about the meaning of self-interest: What was on the worker's mind? The management of labor seemed to depend upon an answer to that question. But the industrial psychologists who proposed to supply that answer were of many minds: Behaviorism and instinct-psychology were competing for attention. The many answers which were given emptied the old-fashioned "pursuit of gain" of such simple meanings as it once had, but they put nothing definite in its place. That was done rather by vocational psychology. The individual worker came to be considered as a conglomerate of traits which could be measured by tests, and these tests could be used in selection and job-placement. This approach was welcomed by employers, who had a job to get done; it mattered little whether the traits it measured were acquired or innate. The tests were admirably suited for the solution of the managerial task. As a manager put it during the 1920's, "The fundamental problem in employment becomes the measurement of the amounts of the traits in each applicant or worker."

But the tests had repercussions of their own, and these led quickly from the measurement of manual skills to the measurement of intangible attitudes. For the abilities of an individual could not be investigated apart from his interests, and these in turn were the result of social and emotional influences inside and outside his place of work. Just when the scientific device of testing appeared to solve the new problems of management in a definitive way, speculation became rife about the motivation of workers. Managers declared that workers wanted to take pride in their work, that they wanted a recognized place in society, a constructive career, a sense of ownership, and so on. By the 1930's this awareness of the workers as "human beings" was widespread. The demand was repeated time and again that their personality and dignity, their attitudes and inner feelings must be respected. Of course, this recognition of the workers' attitudes and feelings was never far removed from the more traditional denunciation of the "great unwashed" as lazy and incapable. Managers had merely to add that they were also unreasonable, sentimental, emotional, tractable, gullible, and deeply desirous of being led by their betters. But for all that, a significant change had occurred. For in the past the worker had been regarded as a man who had to labor for others because he had failed in the struggle for survival, and he had been told to emulate the competitive drive which accounted for the success of his employers. His human features merely corresponded to this subordinate role in the scheme of things. Now, however, much of the verbal imagery dealt with worker's "search for expression and growth."

The new image of the worker was a consequence of many developments such as the fight against trade unions, scientific management, and the increasing complexity of industrial organizations. For the same reasons American employers and managers came to question the basis of their own authority. As they proposed to do something about the workers who did not produce efficiently or cooperate fully, failure would no longer be due to vice and incapacity alone, but to defects of management as well. Henceforth, success was no longer the self-evident result of superiority. Employers were consciously addressing themselves to the task of accomplishing by human interference what the struggle for survival had done automatically before—weeding out the unfit and rewarding the best. And in their attempts to accomplish this end by appropriate managerial policies, they came to discuss the qualities of leadership rather than merely congratulate themselves. "Now that the American worker's mind has been explored," ran a comment in 1924, "one might be led to expect a similar exploration of the mind of management. . . . The mind of management is also an integral part of human relationships in industry."[9] Against those who asserted that great leaders were born and not made, there were others who insisted that they were both born and made, that there were good and bad managers, and that it was necessary to give serious thought to the problems of management. Employers would now prove themselves by skill as well as by success.

The contrast between earlier and later images of "the manager" is easily stated in abstract terms. In the 1840's the "habits of business" were said to include "industry, arrangement, calculation, prudence, punctuality and perseverance."[10] A century later a group of prominent managers listed personal appearance, intelligence, willingness to assume responsibility, self-control, broadmindedness, and decisiveness as the first six of a dozen "executive traits."[11] Vague as these ideal qualities are, they had clearly changed from the image of a man whose success consists in getting things done to one whose success depended upon effective action in a complex, industrial organization.

During the 1920's Dale Carnegie exerted great influence in his inadvertent adaptation of the old ideals to the new realities of large-scale enterprises. His tales of "glorified gossip" about how one man had succeeded and how another had failed, pointed out that "we are evaluated and classified by four things: by what we do, by how we look, by what we say, and how we say it."[12] This instruction in the bureaucratic arts was useful in its way for white-collar workers and even for managers. But for the worker it was clearly beside the point. How he looked and what he said was of no interest to his employer.

In the past the leaders of economic enterprises had been regarded

[9] *American Management Review*, XIII (1924), pp. 6-7.

[10] See Harvey J. Wexler, "How to Succeed in Business, 1840-60," *Explorations in Entrepreneurial History*, I (1949), p. 27.

[11] *The Management Review*, XXVII (1938), p. 303.

[12] Dale Carnegie, *Public Speaking and Influencing Men of Business* (New York: Association Press, 1938), p. 509.

as men whose success spoke for itself. By their superior capacity for perseverance, hard work, prudence, and daring they had come out on top in the struggle for survival. Gradually, however, these leaders became preoccupied with the complex tasks of management. The imagery of their superior virtues changed accordingly from the praise of qualities ideally suited to the competitive struggle to a praise of qualities ideally suited to the management of men and the advancement of bureaucratic careers.

At this point it will be helpful to relate ideology to the environment and organization of American industry. The ideological changes I have traced may be interpreted as managerial response to changes in the organization of industry. Between 1899 and 1947 the number of administrative employees per one hundred production workers in the manufacturing industries of the United States increased from eight to twenty-two.[13] And several studies have shown that this increasing bureaucratization has affected management qualitatively as well as quantitatively. Recruitment of managerial personnel places a heavy emphasis on higher education, managerial tasks have become specialized, organization itself has become a specialty of experts, consultation and committee work are encouraged, the road of advancement through the managerial ranks has lengthened, and so on.[14] The top executives who have been the leading participants in these organizational changes, have become as prominent in their way as the industrial tycoons had been at an earlier time.

But this rise to prestige and power also posed a problem for managerial ideology. The qualities appropriate for the man who wanted to get ahead in the large-scale enterprise were inappropriate in the job the ordinary worker had to do. Thanks to industrial psychology workers were considered only in terms of their attitudes and real wants, not in terms of a struggle for survival and success

[13] See Seymour Melman, "The Rise of Administrative Overhead in the Manufacturing Industries of the United States, 1899-1947," *Oxford Economic Papers,* III (1951), p. 66.

[14] Two comprehensive empirical studies of these organizational changes are now available. See Ernest Dale, *Planning and Developing the Company Structure,* Research Report No. 20 (New York: American Management Association, 1952) and Mabel Newcomer, *The Big Business Executive* (New York: Columbia University Press, 1955).

in which managers and men were judged by the same standard. Of course, workers had never been active participants in the bureaucratic organization of economic enterprises. And it might appear to be a matter of simple logic to exclude them from the appeals which invite those who have a chance to emulate the superior qualities of the leaders. But it had never before been admitted that the worker did not have a chance, that he was excluded from the promise of success. Ideologically, a gulf had opened between the leaders and the led in American industry, which ran counter to every tenet of the American creed.

MANAGERIAL IDEOLOGY AND THE WORK OF ELTON MAYO

It has been the contribution of Elton Mayo, late Professor of Industrial Research at Harvard, to resolve this dilemma. Instead of excluding the worker from the promise of striving and success, Mayo reinterpreted the nature of man. Workers as well as salaried employees and managers could once again be discussed in terms of the same basic human qualities. In the place of the older theories of motivation, Mayo developed an image of man as a creature of sentiments, whose overriding desire was to stand well with his fellows. Managers and workers remained different only in that the former would control their sentiments, develop logical thinking and master the facts of "human relations," while the latter would not. By this reinterpretation Mayo eliminated the praise of virtue and the promise of success from the perspectives of managerial thinking. Henceforth success was identified with the "effective organization" of an enterprise, and the test of success for the individual was his ability to control himself as he controlled others. "The administrator of the future must be able to understand the human-social facts for what they actually are, unfettered by his own emotion or prejudice."[15]

The "human relations" approach has been accepted in practice only partially, for as it solves problems it raises others. Who should undertake the training of a new managerial elite, which Mayo demanded? Should teamwork and management by committees be permitted to crowd out individual initiative and competitiveness? How can technical competence be made compatible with skill in

[15] Elton Mayo, *The Social Problems of an Industrial Civilization* (Boston: Graduate School of Business Administration, Harvard University, 1945), p. 122.

manipulating men? How can future managers be trained without detrimental effects on the organization as a going concern and without giving them too much confidence in their own indispensability? Related questions arise when workers are managed according to the "human relations" approach, for then workers are treated as "victims" of emotional complications rather than as men who want to increase their earnings. Is this a feasible alternative? Can attention to the worker's attitudes be genuine in a hierarchical organization? Is the desire for social prestige as manageable a motive as the desire for money? Given the tradition of competitive striving as well as the growing complexity of managerial problems, it is probable that the practical proposals of this approach have been accepted tentatively and in a variety of ways in keeping with the interests and needs of each enterprise.

These questions should not obscure the fact, however, that during the last twenty years American management has had a rapidly growing interest in "human relations" and has actively supported research in this field. This approach has certainly provided one of the methods by which the increasingly complex problems of management could be approached. In dealing with these problems the growing number of middle-managers may be said to have found an approach congenial which was patterned in the image of their own bureaucratic careers. And this managerial interest has been aided and abetted by an increasing number of social scientists who have found a new and fruitful opportunity for research in studies of "human relations" in industry.

The language of teamwork and loyalty fits in well with the give-and-take of men whose drive to advance on the bureaucratic ladder must be coordinated with the imperatives of getting the work done. The earlier picture of industrial society had contained a division between the successful few and the unsuccessful many which had left no place for the large number of those who belonged to neither group. As the proportion of independent businessmen declined while that of dependent employees increased, it became necessary to accommodate the prevailing images and beliefs to the realities of bureaucratic organizations rather than to the realities of a competitive market. And today, American businessmen face the question whether the collectivism of "human relations" will overtake the individualism of the "strenuous life."

· II ·

MANAGEMENT'S APPROACH TO "HUMAN RELATIONS"

BY JAMES C. WORTHY
Sears, Roebuck and Company

From its inception, the so-called "human relations" movement has been viewed with considerable skepticism and mistrust by persons outside the ranks of management—particularly by leaders of organized labor and by students of labor problems. Those who seek to criticize management on this score, however, find themselves in a difficult position, for obviously they cannot argue against good human relations as such; to do so would be like arguing against virtue. Besides, their own stock in trade has in large part been a protest against management's sins of omission and commission in its relations with its workers, and it sets with little grace for them to attack management for trying to overcome some of the shortcomings for which they themselves have taken management so roundly to task.

There is a curious reversal of roles here which the critics of management find troublesome. By trying to improve worker satisfactions—psychic as well as material—through use of the insights of human relations research, management seems to be moving into an area which its critics have traditionally and temperamentally regarded as peculiarly their own. And in truth, it must be disconcerting for people with a well-staked-out field of interest to find their supposed adversary playing on the same field but with his own equipment and according to his own rules. Something, the critics seem to feel, is radically wrong with this picture of management trying to improve human relations. It is perhaps only human that they should conclude that what is wrong is not so much *what* management is trying to do but *why* management is trying to do it.

Typically, therefore, the attack is on management's motives. Under the common stereotype of management, all managerial action must be in terms of the self-interest of managers and owners, with only such consideration of the interests of workers as may be enforced by law or custom or union regulation, or as may be dictated by a prudent regard for possible adverse consequences. So if management adopts any policy or pursues any course of action, it can be designed for only one purpose: to serve the needs of management, conceived only as broadly as circumstances may require.

So, with human relations—the line of reasoning runs—management cannot be interested in the well-being of its workers but must be seeking more effective means of manipulating and controlling them for its own selfish ends. This effort is seen as particularly heinous for it seems to debase and prostitute the results of scientific research. And precisely because the methods of human relations are to some extent based on validated scientific procedures, they are likely to be more effective in achieving their aims than the traditional rule of thumb devices which management has used in the past. Things were bad enough when management employed straightforward techniques of manipulation and control—even of coercion. But now management is going scientific!

MOTIVATIONS OF MANAGEMENT

But management's interest in human relations is something less than a monstrous plot. There is no denying management has economic motives, that it sees in human relations techniques a means for improving its organization, for reducing friction at the workplace, for increasing quantity and quality of output, for reducing costs. Management is concerned with such matters; after all, they are among the primary functions of management, and if the application of human relations concepts promises to aid in their achievement, management can hardly be blamed for wanting to use them. Nor has management ever sought to disguise the utilitarian aspects of human relations: quite the contrary. If anything, it has overemphasized such aspects and thereby oversimplified its real motivation.

One of the early and most significant of the findings of human relations research was that workers are not motivated solely by economic considerations, that there are many so-called "nonlogical" factors (i.e., non*economically-logical factors*) which strongly condition their attitudes and behavior. It is curious that this insight has never been extended in any important way to management, that while it is now axiomatic that workers are complex and many-sided, management is still seen as the corporate embodiment of economic man. But if the motivations of workers are complex and often "nonlogical," the motivations of managers are hardly less so. Managers no less than workers are members of groups that strongly influence their behavior, play roles that are socially defined, are members of a culture with a rich and elaborate system of values. Managers no more than workers are motivated solely by economic considerations. Not that economic considerations are unimportant in either case, but other factors of great significance are likewise at work. Managers, in a word, are "human," too.

One characteristic of managers is a concern for good relations with their employees, partly because such relations are considered important from the standpoint of the economic aims of the enterprise, but partly for other and considerably more complex reasons as well. This is not to suggest that all managements strive to maintain good employee relations at all times, nor even that those who do so strive are consistently successful in their efforts. Nevertheless, the record is reasonably clear that, by and large, American management has shown a marked concern for good employee relations, for reasons growing out of certain peculiarities in the history and traditions of this country.

CHRONIC LABOR SCARCITY

For one thing, American business enterprise has been faced with a persistent shortage of labor from Colonial days forward. Whereas in other countries (for example, Great Britain a century and a half ago and India today) industrialization has generally arisen under conditions of large-scale labor surplus, American managers, with only occasional and temporary exceptions, have had to build and maintain their enterprises in the face of chronic labor scarcity. The special American penchant for mechanization reflects the need for conserving the available supply of labor. The special American genius for organization reflects the need for utilizing scarce skills in the most effective manner possible. Likewise, the special American concern for maintaining good relations with employees undoubtedly reflects the necessity for making employment as attractive as possible to people who are in a position to pick and choose among places of work.

It makes a profound difference—psychological as well as technical—whether workers are easily come by or hard to find and keep. Scarcity always enhances value—and respect. And that which is valued and respected is better cared for, particularly when lack of care may lead to loss. Scarcity has conditioned the minds of workers as well as managers. Just as American workers have grown to expect and demand good wages, they have grown to expect and demand good treatment. This, too, has strongly conditioned the thinking of realistic managers.

Without doubt, stringency in the supply of labor has been one of the highly significant factors in the development of American capitalism which has tended to differentiate it markedly from the capitalism of other countries. This aspect of American industrial history deserves far more study than has yet been given it. Particularly deserving of study is the manner in which labor scarcity has helped mold the psychological and cultural climate of American industrial society and the attitudes and practices of American industrial managers.

AUTHORITY IN AN EGALITARIAN SOCIETY

Other and more subtle factors have helped sharpen still further the interest of American managers in the quality of their employee relations. One of these is a rather ambivalent attitude toward the authoritarian role they must play in the hierarchy of industrial organization.

The lack of a high degree of social stratification in this country, the relative ease with which people have been able to move from one social class to another, and above all the strong egalitarian elements in American culture have tended to deprive members of the managerial group of a full sense of sureness in the rightness of their authority in relation to their subordinates. Where lines between social classes are more definitely drawn, authority tends to be exercised as a matter of unquestioned right, and to be so accepted by the workers themselves. Americans, on the contrary, are likely to be troubled by vague feelings of unease when placed in positions where they must behave in ways of superiority toward other Americans who by all standards of the American tradition are their equals and whose position of inferiority in the business enterprise in no way detracts from their essential equality as citizens and men.

This unease helps explain the peculiar sensitivity of the American employer to what his employees think of him—as expressed, for example, in his widespread use of such devices as "morale surveys" and employee opinion polls. But while this sensitivity and the use of such devices may be a source of wonder or amusement to foreign observers, they reflect an important characteristic of American industrial life: the conflict between a deep-seated egalitarianism and the functional necessity for a certain degree of authoritarianism in relationships within the industrial organization.

These feelings of unease are likely to be particularly strong when "good native Americans" find themselves in positions of authority over other "good native Americans." The same compunctions are often strikingly absent, by contrast, when the same "good native Americans" are in positions of authority over less favored groups, such as Negroes or immigrants. Here the "good native American" is likely to feel secure in his superiority and to have few qualms about the "rightness" and "naturalness" of his authority. In such relationships, the American manager is more likely to think and act in ways similar to his counterparts in other societies which take for granted the prerogatives of members of "superior" classes to command their "inferiors." Superordination in such cases is not merely functional; it implies and assumes that the superiors are also better *men.*

INFLUENCE OF IMMIGRATION

This tendency to differentiate in attitudes toward subordinates according to their social and ethnic characteristics goes far toward explaining some of the seeming contradictions in the history of

American industrial relations. For despite the concern for employee good will postulated above as a distinguishing feature of American management, this country has been torn by some of the bloodiest and most intractable labor strife of any modern nation. Much of this strife has arisen, however, in industries which have employed large numbers of immigrant laborers: steel, mining, lumber, and automobiles, to name only a few. Here, the inevitable stresses and strains of emerging large-scale enterprise and the equally inevitable conflicts of economic interest were further and often intolerably aggravated by the conflict of cultures, the lack of adequate means of communication, and above all, a widespread feeling on the part of owners and managers—who were likely to be "good native Americans"—that their laborers were "naturally" inferior.

All this, however, was a passing phase, at least so far as the European immigrants were concerned. It continues to exist with respect to Negroes, Japanese, and others whose achievement of status as "good native Americans" is seriously impeded by visible racial differences still read by Americans, in their current conventions, as imposing barriers to acceptance which even the most thorough acculturation cannot dissolve. But the great tide of European immigration has been cut off for more than a generation. The proportion of foreign-born workers in the population is declining rapidly, and even "first generation Americans" no longer occupy the fairly conspicuous place they once did. Second and third generation Americans are thoroughly acculturated, with only the most tenuous connection or identification with the countries of their ancestral origin. The "melting pot" has done its work well. Names like Larson, O'Rourke, and Emmerick have long been as good as Adams, Burgess, and Townsend; names like Novak, Pagano, and Nemechek are acquiring an easy familiarity. And the same compunctions that through our history have fostered a degree of circumspection in the behavior of an Adams toward a Barker, and a couple of generations ago tempered his behavior toward a Baehr, now conditions his behavior toward a Bielski.

One wonders what would have been the course of American labor history—and the state of labor relations in the United States today—if, during the formative years of modern American industry, the labor force had been largely composed of the same "good native

American" stock that so largely comprised the owning and managing groups. One suspects that the history would have been quite different than it was, and the present state of labor relations would be quite different than it is. For the tide of immigration left its mark, and many features of management thinking and practice which have had so unfortunate an influence on the course and character of American labor relations had their origin in the period when much of the labor force of the emerging large-scale industry was composed of "obviously inferior" breeds of men. Given the egalitarian American tradition, restrictive in its scope as it undoubtedly was, matters would probably have been much different if workers as well as owners and managers had been "good native Americans" all.

But now the wheel of history has turned another full cycle, and the sons and grandsons and great grandsons of the once "inferior breeds" are fully as "good" and "native" and "American" as those of the men for whom their forebears worked. And their bosses are beset by the same feelings of diffidence which have generally characterized those imbued with the egalitarian American tradition when placed in positions of functional superiority over their "equals." It is not without significance that the modern "science of human relations," which has won such wide attention in management circles, first emerged in the mid-thirties—which was about the time the last wave of immigration began to be fully digested.

RISE OF ORGANIZED LABOR

Neither is it without significance that at this same time the labor movement in this country entered into the period of phenomenal growth which has made it so powerful a factor in modern industrial life. For the labor force was no longer composed in important parts of Bohunks and Polacks and Wops, but of people who had acquired the elements of American culture, who demanded to be treated as self-respecting, upstanding American citizens, and who found their deepest sentiments violated by management attitudes and practices which were a carryover from an earlier period. And so, as self-reliant American citizens, they revolted and sought to create through the device of unions the means for enforcing respect and consideration.

This is not the place to examine the extent to which the union movement may have been an effective means for this purpose or the extent to which in achieving emancipation from one form of arbitrary authority the workers may now find themselves subjected to another. Suffice it for our purposes to note that this "revolt of labor" was deeply shocking to management. Among other things, it hastened the change in management's attitudes, which was already under way but which had not moved quite fast enough to keep pace with the substantially complete "Americanization" of the labor force that so closely followed the closing of the doors of immigration. Suffice it to note, too, that the emergence of a powerful union movement provided a further incentive to management to take stock of the quality of its employee relations.

QUEST FOR BETTER WAYS OF LIFE

But the external pressures of the union movement, the exigencies of competing for a scarce supply of labor, and a peculiar sensitivity to worker attitudes growing out of the egalitarian American tradition do not entirely explain the special concern for good employee relations which is characteristic of American management. To these must be added management's own search for a better way of life for itself and its employees.

American history from its earliest beginnings has been instinct with the search for better ways of life—not merely better ways of earning a livelihood but better ways of *living*. This applies not only to the early settlers, not only to those who fought the Revolution, founded the Republic, and preserved the Union: it continues to this day as one of the strong, persistent themes in American history and a distinguishing characteristic of American society. American management is an integral part of that society and shares that characteristic.

One expression of this is the value placed on being "a good employer." The public evaluation of an enterprise is often based largely on its reputation in this respect. Businessmen take pride in having their firms known as "good places to work," not only by workers but by the general public and their fellow businessmen; in formulating their business policies, they are likely to take this factor very much into account. This is not a new development but a feature of our entire industrial history.

This historical theme has been expressed in a variety of ways: in utopian ventures a century and more ago to "uplift" the economic and intellectual status of workers, in the development of the now outmoded concept of "welfare capitalism," in the introduction of a wide variety of employee benefit plans—group insurance and hospitalization, profit sharing, paid vacations and holidays, retirement allowances, paid sick leave, regularized employment, and a host of other measures designed to provide greater present and future security for workers and their families. Measures such as these were not the inventions of the unions; they were originally developed and installed by managements, usually at their own initiative and of their own free will, in an effort to assist in meeting the needs of workers in modern industrial society. The unions have taken these plans over as their own and considerably extended their application, but in doing so they have merely followed a pattern already well established by progressive, forward-looking managements.

RECONCILIATION OF ROLES

In developing plans such as these, management has been motivated by more than economic self-interest, although it has managed effectively to disguise that fact even from itself. For under the accepted canons of business enterprise, businessmen (including managers) are *supposed* to act only in terms of monetary considerations. Everything they do is expected to pass the test of whether and how much it contributes to profits. The businessman's and the manager's role is very clearly defined in these terms not only by themselves but by the society of which they are a part.

Actually, they seldom carry out literally the injunctions of their official creed. As with workers, owners and managers have never acted strictly in the terms of narrow self-interest ascribed to them by economic theory. There has always been a system of *human* relations as well as a system of *economic* relations. The two systems function in terms of two different and sometimes conflicting sets of values, with the result that there is often confusion as to the role the businessman is actually playing at any particular time.

It is amusing to observe the extent to which the businessman will sometimes go in his efforts to explain in terms of self-interest an action which he wants to take for perhaps quite different reasons, some of which may be definitely generous and unselfish. But because generosity and unselfishness are explicitly outside the frame of reference within which the businessman, *as a businessman,* is supposed to operate, he feels it necessary to explain himself in other terms. One such term is likely to be "enlightened self-interest." One suspects that the frequency with which *enlightened* self-interest is appealed to reflects the difficulty of relating certain acts to self-interest at all, and that the adjective "enlightened" serves merely to suggest a relationship that might be exceedingly difficult to trace out in detail.

In any event, the justification of generous acts in terms of self-interest, whether "enlightened" or otherwise, helps soothe the businessman's conscience for acting contrary to his socially defined role—or, perhaps more accurately, helps reconcile the requirements of his role as a businessman and the requirements of his role as a citizen. The businessman's role in society is much more complex than his business role alone, and very often other and conflicting roles take over in what may appear to be strictly business situations. But when this happens, the businessman is likely to find himself very uncomfortable unless he can find a way of explaining his actions as really selfish after all. Under these circumstances, the device of *enlightened* self-interest is a useful one indeed.

This circumlocution also helps make the action more palatable to those who benefit from it. Workers would be very suspicious if the act were presented as anything other than self-interest. They, too, know the behavior appropriate to management's role and are likely to feel uncomfortable—and perhaps resentful—unless the behavior is carefully defined in terms of that role. Their own role as workers, in turn, makes them dislike being indebted to management for favors. Presenting the act as merely selfish behavior on management's part thus gets better acceptance than if it were presented in some other guise. The situation reminds one of a doting father and a loving son who go to great lengths of gruffness to hide their affection for each other and who would be fearfully embarrassed if that affection should ever inadvertently be expressed in words.

CONCLUSION

The special concern of American businessmen and managers for good employee relations may thus be accounted for in a variety of ways. It springs in part from factors which may be grouped broadly under the heading of self-interest, with or without the adjective "enlightened": the need to reduce friction and promote teamwork as an aid to efficient production, competition for workers in a tight labor market, the pressure of a strong labor movement. But it owes its unique character to factors which transcend any realistic definition of self-interest: the egalitarian American tradition, and the simple desire of those in strategic positions within the business system to create an industrial way of life that comports more nearly with their sense of the fitness of things.

Given this background, the interest of American management in the science of human relations is readily understandable. Human relations was by no means the first—and certainly will not be the last—of the methods adopted by management to promote better relationships with its employees.

· III ·

HUMAN RELATIONS IN THE WORKPLACE: AN APPRAISAL OF SOME RECENT RESEARCH*

BY HAROLD L. WILENSKY
University of Michigan

This paper is an attempt to state and subject to sociological appraisal the findings of some recent American social research on human relations in industry. It aims to do this in a way that will permit discussion of the relation of the social scientist to the practitioner.

This research has been extensively, ably, and repetitively summarized and overviewed[1] and criticized.[2] "Human relations in in-

* Revision of paper presented in part at the Seventh Annual Meeting of the Industrial Relations Research Association, Detroit, December 29, 1954. I wish to acknowledge the helpful suggestions of Professors Guy E. Swanson and Daniel Katz of the University of Michigan, and Dr. Erving Goffman of the National Institute of Mental Health.

[1] Among the best summary articles and volumes: C. M. Arensberg in *Social Psychology at the Crossroads*, J. H. Rohrer and M. Sherif, eds. (New York: Harper, 1951), pp. 324-352; W. F. Whyte in *ibid.*, pp. 297-312; D. Katz, "An Overview of the Human Relations Program," and R. L. Kahn, "An Analysis of Supervisory Practices and Components of Morale," in *Groups, Leadership and Men*, H. Guetzkow, ed. (Pittsburgh: Carnegie Press, 1951), pp. 68-89; D. Katz and R. L. Kahn, "Some Recent Findings in Human Relations Research in Industry," in *Readings in Social Psychology*, G. E. Swanson, T. M. Newcomb, and E. L. Hartley, eds. (Rev. ed.; New York: Holt, 1952), pp. 650-665; R. L. Kahn and D. Katz, "Leadership Practices in Relation to Productivity and Morale," in *Group Dynamics*, D. Cartwright and A. Zander, eds. (Evanston,

dustry" as discussed and attacked in both academic and nonacademic publications has become a rather loose phrase. Sometimes it seems

---

Ill.: Row, Peterson, 1953), pp. 612-628; D. Katz and R. L. Kahn, "Human Organization and Worker Motivation," in *Industrial Productivity* (Madison: Industrial Relations Research Association, 1951), pp. 146-171; D. Katz, "Satisfactions and Deprivations in Industrial Life," in *Industrial Conflict*, A. Kornhauser, R. Dubin, and A. M. Ross, eds. (New York: McGraw-Hill, 1954), pp. 86-106; M. S. Viteles, *Motivation and Morale in Industry* (New York: Norton, 1953); C. Argyris, "The Present State of Research in Human Relations in Industry: A Working Paper," mimeographed (New Haven: Labor and Management Center, Yale University, March 1, 1954). Among the most useful readers and texts: R. Dubin, *Human Relations in Administration* (New York: Prentice-Hall, 1951); R. K. Merton, A. P. Gray, B. Hockey, and H. C. Selvin, eds., *Reader in Bureaucracy* (Glencoe, Ill.: Free Press, 1952); Cartwright and Zander, eds., *Group Dynamics, op. cit.*; D. C. Miller and W. H. Form, *Industrial Sociology: An Introduction to the Sociology of Work Relations* (New York: Harper, 1951); T. Caplow, *The Sociology of Work* (Minneapolis: University of Minnesota Press, 1954); H. Simon, D. W. Smithburg, and V. A. Thompson, *Public Administration* (New York: Knopf, 1951).

[2] Among the best critical articles: D. Bell, "Adjusting Men to Machines," *Commentary*, III (January-June 1947), pp. 79-88; H. Blumer, "Sociological Theory in Industrial Relations," *American Sociological Review*, XII (June 1947), pp. 271-278; H. Sheppard, "Managerial Sociology" (Doctoral dissertation, University of Wisconsin, 1948) and "Approaches to Conflict in American Industrial Sociology," *The British Journal of Sociology*, V (December 1954), pp. 324-341; W. E. Moore, "Industrial Sociology: Status and Prospects," *American Sociological Review*, XIII (August 1948), pp. 382-391; C. W. Mills, "The Contribution of Sociology to Studies of Industrial Relations," in *Proceedings of the First Annual Meeting, December 29-30, 1948* (Champaign: Industrial Relations Research Association, 1949), pp. 199-222; [L. Carliner] "Deep Therapy on the Assembly Line: Moo, moo, moo, say the cow sociologists, but they don't even give skimmed milk," *Ammunition*, VII (April 1949), pp. 47-51; A. Kornhauser, "Introduction," in *Psychology of Labor-Management Relations* (Champaign: Industrial Relations Research Association, 1949), pp. 1-5; R. Bendix and L. H. Fisher, "The Perspectives of Elton Mayo," *Review of Economics and Statistics*, XXXI (November 1949), p. 317; W. Koivisto, "Value, Theory, and Fact in Industrial Sociology," *The American Journal of Sociology*, LVIII (May 1953), pp. 564-572; C. Kerr, "What Became of the Independent Spirit?" *Fortune*, XLVIII (July 1953), pp. 110-111. Cf. R. C. Stone, "Conflicting Approaches to the Study of Worker-Manager Relations," *Social Forces*, XXXI (December 1952), pp. 117-124. Flogging the human relations researchers for uncritically or unconsciously accepting management's view of the worker as a means to be manipulated toward an impersonal end, that of productive efficiency, and hence profits; flogging these researchers again for their love of order, harmony, and stability, and their low-rating of the values of equality and freedom of association (with its attendant conflict)—this has indeed become an international sport, with the latest plays by Friedmann in France and Richmond in England. G. Friedmann, *Ou va le Travail Humain?* (Paris: Gallimard, 1950) and A. H. Richmond, "Conflict and Authority in Industry," *Occupational Psychology*, XXVIII (January 1954), pp. 24-33.

to mean all of social science outside of economics—an unnecessarily ambitious view. Sometimes it seems to confine the focus of study to manual workers in manufacturing plants—an unnecessarily narrow view. For purposes of this paper I shall define the area as the study of the social relations of people at work. The central problem: social and social psychological aspects of the organization of work and the nature of work experience in urban-industrial society. The object of study: people at work taking account of each other in typical ways.

I will not try to summarize small slices of the literature of "human relations in industry" as defined above. Instead I will make two points I think are sometimes overlooked by its producers, its critics, and its consumers alike:

1. Not everything the social scientist does is of use to the practitioner —and maybe this is a good thing.

2. There are at least three things beyond the value orientation of the investigator that seem to account for some dominant tendencies in human relations research: (a) the time perspective and historical sensitivity of the researcher; (b) how much attention he pays to the urban industrial settings; and (related to this) (c) the extent to which he is preoccupied with psychological variables.

I will try to illustrate these points with some of the themes that have run through the American research since Mayo.

SOCIAL SCIENCE AND SOCIAL PRACTICE

My first major point is obvious but perhaps because of this, it is sometimes overlooked. It should be stated frequently: *not everything done by the social scientist can or should help the practitioner.* To illustrate, I would like first to consider some examples of social research which gets close attention from business leaders. Then I would like to mention some research questions that do not excite business leaders at all or for that matter the leaders of any interest group, but which nevertheless have both theoretical and social relevance.

Applying Some Generalizations

Take the problem of the literate business leader or company staff expert who looks to the academic social scientist for help. There is much research which, whatever its contribution to social science theory, is eminently practical. Our business leader may first come across some observations about size of group and human conduct. It is an ancient sociological generalization, e.g., that size of immediate work group is negatively correlated with productivity, or job satisfaction, or regular attendance, or industrial peace—other factors being equal.[3] This is due in part to the greater likelihood that primary relations (relations that are intimate, personal, inclusive, and experienced as spontaneous) are more likely to develop in small groups than in large groups. It is due in part also to the fact that the worker in the smaller group is likely to have more knowledge of the relation between effort and earnings, and this seems to increase his incentive to work.[4]

But our business leader might then note the considerable evidence—also a product of careful research—that these intimate groups and grouplets in the workplace at given times and places act as effective saboteurs of management aims and expectations. These groups may offer their members a greater sense of belonging and a better knowledge of production processes and results, but they may use both loyalty and knowledge to resist management control and direction.[5]

[3] See C. C. Balderston, *Group Incentives* (Philadelphia: University of Pennsylvania Press, 1930), pp. 128-163; Z. C. Dickinson, *Compensating Industrial Effort* (New York: Ronald Press, 1937), pp. 260-290; R. Marriott, "Size of Working Group and Output," *Occupational Psychology*, XXIII (January 1949), pp. 47-57; D. Katz, "Morale and Motivation in Industry," in *Current Trends in Industrial Psychology* (Pittsburgh: University of Pittsburgh Press, 1949), p. 168. Cf. D. Katz, "Survey Research Center: An Overview of the Research Program," in Guetzkow, ed., *Groups, Leadership and Men, op. cit.*, p. 81. Over half a century ago, Emile Durkheim observed in France that "small-scale industry, where work is less divided, displays a relative harmony between worker and employer. It is only in large-scale industry," he complained, "that these relations are in a sickly state." *The Division of Labor in Society* (Glencoe, Ill.: Free Press, 1947), p. 356.

[4] See evidence cited in Viteles, *op. cit.*, pp. 140 ff.

[5] Among many studies on this point see S. B. Mathewson, *Restriction of Output Among Unorganized Workers* (New York: Viking, 1931); F. Roethlisberger and W. Dickson, *Management and the Worker* (Cambridge: Harvard University Press, 1939); D. Roy, "Quota Restriction and Goldbricking in a Machine Shop," *American Journal of Sociology*, LVII (March 1952), pp. 427-442; O. Collins, M. Dalton, and D. Roy, "Restriction of Output and Social Cleavage in Industry," *Applied Anthropology*, V (Summer 1946), pp. 1-14. The formidable set of sanctions which enforce work group solidarity are well

Given this apparent contradiction—small work group size means greater organizational effectiveness, small work groups are subversive of organizational aims—the business leader can turn to a third set of studies. These studies show that under some circumstances the small work group can be utilized, can strengthen the big organization. But how and under what circumstances?

There are at least three answers to that question suggested by current research—answers which emphasize one of three variables: (1) the degree of identification of work group members with the larger organization and its goals; (2) the supervisor's leadership style; or (3) the degree of diffusion of authority in the organization. I am not sure that any of these answers offers much comfort to the business leader who wants help.

One set of researches—mainly, but not exclusively, studies of Army life by the Stouffer team in World War II—suggests this proposition: strong primary group solidarity can function to strengthen the large formal organization and encourage greater conformity to its directives when (1) there is a predisposing general sense of obligation to the larger purpose of the organization and a readiness to acknowledge the leader's right to command (the soldier in battle, e.g., accepts in some minimum degree the necessity of winning the war and the legitimacy of his superior's directives toward that end); and (2) there is strong opposition to the achievement of this goal from the outside (e.g., an enemy nation). Here the sanctions of the informal group (e.g., "don't let your buddies down or you'll be an outcast"), the sanctions of the formal organization (e.g., "you'll be court-martialed if you desert"), and moral considerations ("this is my patriotic duty") all work in the same direction—i.e., toward high "productivity" (in the Army, effective combat performance).[6]

---

illustrated in this latter study. Aside from being subject to ridicule, social ostracism, hiding of tools, and threat of injury, the nonconforming machinist (who fails to restrict output in accordance with work group norms) is denied access to a series of trade secrets by which his work life would be made easy: e.g., methods of "making out" on "tight jobs" unknown to the industrial engineers, deceptive devices for looking busy during a time study, useful inventions made on company time and concealed from management—special cutting tools, jigs, and fixtures, etc. *Ibid.*, pp. 8-9.

[6] Cf. Edward A. Shils' careful critical analysis of research on the primary group in D. Lerner, H. S. Lasswell, *et al.*, eds., *The Policy Sciences* (Stanford:

A patriotic spirit sustained by approval and affection from his buddies—this moved the German or American soldier to fight in the face of adversity; it even moved Mayo's aircraft workers to stay on the defense job in California. But what has this got to do with our business leader's problem today? When the entity for patriotism is a business enterprise producing for its peacetime profit, and the buddies have less of a sense of the manager's right to command and more of a sense that the manager is playing on a different team —the generalization about identity with the organization and its goals becomes somewhat irrelevant to the problem. The problem from the manager's point of view is to bend the informal work group to the purposes of the enterprise. We tell him that high "group identification" or "group cohesion" or "informal group solidarity" or "pride in work group" or "team spirit" or "group belongingness" or "pride-in-performance of work group" is positively related to productivity and to satisfaction with the company.[7] If by group "identification" we mean identification with company goals as is sometimes the case, then all we have is a tautology: acceptance of company goals causes willingness to conform to company desires —to produce with appropriate enthusiasm. If on the other hand when we say a man is "identified with the group" we mean he accepts the standards and controls of the group and sees the group as a symbol of his values and goals, then we are back where we started: such group identification is expressed as much in slow-

---

Stanford University Press, 1951), pp. 44-69. His essay in R. K. Merton and P. F. Lazarsfeld, eds., *Studies in the Scope and Method of "The American Soldier"* (Glencoe, Ill.: Free Press, 1950), pp. 16-39, summarizes the data on primary groups in the American Army. Compare E. A. Shils and M. Janowitz, "Cohesion and Disintegration in the Wehrmacht in World War II," *Public Opinion Quarterly*, XII (Summer 1948), pp. 280-315; and E. Mayo and G. F. F. Lombard, *Teamwork and Labor Turnover in the Aircraft Industry of Southern California*, Business Research Studies, No. 32 (Boston: Graduate School of Business Administration, Harvard University, 1944), an analysis of the relation of primary group solidarity and induction methods to absenteeism and turnover in two large defense plants in World War II.

[7] The quoted phrases have been used interchangeably in the literature reporting such relationships. See, e.g., Katz and Kahn, "Human Organization and Worker Motivation," *op. cit.*, pp. 161-162; Katz and Kahn, "Some Recent Findings in Human Relations Research in Industry," *op. cit.*, pp. 661-663; N. C. Morse, *Satisfactions in the White Collar Job* (Ann Arbor: Survey Research Center, University of Michigan, 1953), pp. 17-18, 158-160, 188-191.

downs, goldbricking, and general hell-raising as it is in neat conformity to management directives. And the circumstances under which the informal work group falls in line are often beyond the control of the business leader—a point I shall come to in a moment.

If our business friend is by now tired of "identification with the larger organization and its goals" as a variable in performance, he can move to another group of studies—more numerous and varied—which point to the supervisor's leadership style as a key to company utilization of the informal work group. Don't look to intrinsic job satisfaction, don't look to attitudes toward the company, the pay, or job status, these studies tell us; look instead to the way the supervisors exercise their authority. Since the elaborately careful experiments of the Kurt Lewin group with children,[8] it has been noted again and again in a variety of work groups and in varied settings that the more "authoritarian" leaders have a disintegrative effect on group structure and performance.[9] The supervisor in the better-producing work unit "differentiates his role" (e.g., spends more time planning, training, etc., less doing the work the men do); he is "employee-centered" rather than "production-centered" (e.g., takes a personal interest in the men, is understanding, not punitive, when they make mistakes, sides with the men, etc.); and he avoids "close supervision" (e.g., breathing down the necks of the men).[10] This is the leadership style that pays off.

[8] K. Lewin and R. Lippitt, "An Experimental Study of the Effect of Democratic and Authoritarian Group Atmospheres," in Lewin, Lippitt, and Escalona, *Studies in Topological and Vector Psychology*, Part I ("University of Iowa Studies in Child Welfare," XVI, No. 3); R. Lippitt and R. K. White, "The Social Climate of Children's Groups," in R. G. Barker, J. S. Kounin, and H. F. Wright, *Child Behavior and Development* (New York: McGraw-Hill, 1943), pp. 485-508. The latter study is also in Cartwright and Zander, *Group Dynamics*,, *op. cit.*, Chap. 40. In contrast to "authoritarian" or "laissez-faire" leaders, the "democratic" leader encouraged group discussion and decision, made suggestions instead of issuing orders, left the division of work up to the group, was "objective" or "fact-minded" instead of "personal" in praise and criticism, and "tried to be a group member in spirit without doing too much of the work."

[9] See, e.g., the study by Preston and Heintz and those reported by Kahn and Katz in Cartwright and Zander, eds., *Group Dynamics, op. cit.*, Chaps. 39 and 41, respectively.

[10] Ibid., pp. 613-623. Cf. A. Gouldner, *Wildcat Strike* (Yellow Springs, O.: Antioch Press, 1954), who reports that, when new management in the gypsum factory he studied changed the traditional "indulgency pattern" and began "close supervision," the workers staged a wildcat strike.

Here again, though, our social science-using business leader must tread with caution. The evidence, as in much good social research, is uncertain and the generalizations need important qualification. The researchers to their credit make this abundantly clear. A study of nonunion white-collar workers in an insurance company notes that while four sections under general (as opposed to close) supervision had high productivity, one had low productivity.[11] A study of unionized maintenance-of-way railroad workers finds no relationship at all between closeness of supervision and productivity.[12] In the case of the office workers the deviant section (where there was permissive, general supervision but low productivity) is one where the work is very routine. It is suggested here that general supervision will not be effective where the actual process of production is routine. On the other hand, when it comes to explaining the lack of payoff of permissive leadership with railroad gangs, the same researchers point to the fact that railroad work is *less* routine and the work groups are small enough to allow the foreman, via close supervision, "to give each man the benefit of his superior knowledge, and to contribute to the effective performance of his men."[13] In one case, the *routine* work process (deviant section of office workers) is used to explain the failure of general permissive leadership; in the other case, the *non*routine work process (railroad workers) is used to explain the failure of permissive leadership.[14]

[11] "In other words there is no more than a general trend in the direction of greater productivity under general supervision. Similarly, the pride-in-performance index scores for sections appear to be only slightly related to general-close supervision." Morse, *op. cit.*, p. 137.

[12] Survey Research Center, *Productivity, Supervision and Morale Among Railroad Workers,* Human Relations, Series 2, Report 3 (Ann Arbor: The Center, University of Michigan, May 1950), p. 51.

[13] *Ibid.*, p. 52.

[14] In fairness, I should point out that (1) the differences in section productivity in the insurance company were not great; (2) the original reports of research often remind the reader that the indices and measuring instruments used to get at leadership style are not infallible (e.g., these were not observations of on-the-job conduct but self-reported leadership practices coupled with interviewer judgments). Comparing the two studies, the authors suggest that what we are dealing with here is the extent to which the work process permits "contribution of a technical nature from close . . . supervision" (non-routine railroad work, yes; routine insurance office work, no). The discussion at that point seems to slide away from the question of "closeness" and back into the question of "differentiation of role" (effective supervisors spend more time planning, directing, and "performing specific highly skilled tasks"—including, presumably, "technical" contributions). *Ibid.*, pp. 52, 50.

Some of these qualifications and contradictions on the effects of leadership style have led the researchers to a third variable: the control structure of the company or the degree of diffusion of authority. It is in this literature that we hear most often about "consultative leadership," "autonomous work groups," "work group participation," "self-expression and self-determination," "downward delegation," "local autonomy," and the like.[15]

Our generalizations on the effect of diffusion of authority, however, also seem to me to be tenuous. I have made up a chart which compares nine of these studies (the last nine in footnote 15), giving their description of both workplace and environmental variables—type of company or industry, type of work, union status, external market situation, social-cultural background of workers, etc., and how "participation" was related in each study to performance and/or satisfaction. The chart suggests first that "participation" has had both positive and neutral or negative effects in workplaces which are both union and nonunion, big and small, prosperous and marginal—and among employees at all social class levels. But it also suggests that insufficient data have been reported on (1) *type of union* (how militant, how tame, etc.); (2) *structure and character*

[15] H. H. Carey, "Consultative Supervision and Management," *Personnel*, XVIII (March 1942), pp. 286-295; L. Bradford and R. Lippitt, "Building a Democratic Work Group," *Personnel*, XXII (November 1945), pp. 142-152; J. C. Worthy, "Factors Influencing Employee Morale," *Harvard Business Review*, XXVIII (January 1950), pp. 61-73; Katz and Kahn in Swanson, Newcomb, and Hartley, eds., *Readings in Social Psychology, op. cit.*, especially pp. 663-664, and in *Industrial Productivity, op. cit.*, pp. 168-171; Katz in Kornhauser, Dubin, and Ross, eds., *Industrial Conflict, op. cit.*, pp. 100-106; Babchuck and Goode, *op. cit.*; L. Coch and J. R. P. French, Jr., "Overcoming Resistance to Change," in Swanson, Newcomb, and Hartley, eds., *Readings in Social Psychology, op. cit.*, pp. 474-491; Morse, *op. cit.*; D. Katz, N. Maccoby, and N. C. Morse, *Productivity, Supervision and Morale in an Office Situation*, Part I (Ann Arbor: Survey Research Center, University of Michigan, December 1950); N. C. Morse, E. Reimer, and A. Tannenbaum, "Change in Control Processes in Social Organization: A Field Experiment," symposium presented at American Psychological Association meetings, New York, September 1954; R. C. Davis, "Factors Related to Scientific Research Performance," in *Interpersonal Factors in Research*, Part I (Ann Arbor: Survey Research Center, University of Michigan, October 1954), Chap. 1; Marquis *et al.*, in Guetzkow, ed., *Groups, Leadership and Men, op. cit.*; J. Levine and J. Butler, "Lecture vs. Group Decision in Changing Behavior," *Journal of Applied Psychology*, XXXVI (February 1952), pp. 29-33; W. H. Scott, *Industrial Leadership and Consultation: A Study of Human Relations in Three Merseyside Firms* (Liverpool: University Press of Liverpool, 1952); A. Bavelas' research reported by K. Lewin, "Frontiers in Group Dynamics," *Human Relations*, I (June 1947), pp. 5-41.

of local labor markets (allegations that lack of participation makes for high turnover and low morale might well indicate the alternative opportunities available to the employees); (3) *product markets* (in one study of department store salesmen, as the authors incidentally note, the wartime boom alone could have accounted for increased productivity, since productivity was measured by clothing sales); and (4) *class identification and mobility aspirations* (the effect of participation programs might be different with young rural girls on their first job in a small pajama factory than on hard-bitten men with long industrial experience and identification with the "working class" and/or a strong union).

All this suggests that, at minimum, the practitioner who wants to apply the human relations research has no clear directive as to what to do—and this is true not only of the findings on size of immediate work group, the character of informal work group solidarity, degree of identification with company goals, and type of leadership style as related to productivity; it applies also to the findings on the relation of "morale" (i.e., satisfaction with job and with company) to all of these variables. The evidence is typically inconclusive, the interpretations sometimes contradictory.[16]

[16] Some studies have confirmed a dictum of popular folklore: contented workers produce more. E.g., D. Katz and H. Hyman, studying five wartime shipyards, found that worker morale (job satisfaction) and productivity were positively related. They suggest that this is a relationship of "circular reinforcement" rooted in in-plant, not out-plant, conditions. "Morale in War Industries," in *Readings in Social Psychology,* T. M. Newcomb and E. L. Hartley, eds. (1st ed.; New York: Holt, 1947), pp. 437-447. Much patient research effort suggests caution in generalizing these findings. A study of human relations in a naval research laboratory notes that a permissively-led, high-morale, well-satisfied group produced no more and possibly less in accordance with management standards than a "restrictively"-led, low-morale group. I. R. Weschler, M. Kahane, and R. Tannenbaum, "Job Satisfaction, Productivitiy and Morale: A Case Study," *Occupational Psychology,* XXVI (January 1952), pp. 1-14. Cf. N. Babchuck and W. J. Goode, "Work Incentives in a Self-Determined Group," *American Sociological Review,* XVI (October 1951), pp. 679-687, and the research of the University of Michigan Survey Research Center reported by Katz and Kahn. Compare the conclusions of a study of 72 small decision-making conferences in industry, business, and government: no relationship between "spread of participation" and satisfaction with meeting and decision, but definite positive association between amount of leader formality or procedural structuring and member satisfaction. D. G. Marquis, H. Guetzkow, and R. W. Heyns in Guetzkow, ed., *Groups, Leadership and Men, op. cit.,* pp. 55-67. These studies suggest the probable conditions under which both low morale

Even when the social scientist turns his attentions to the practical concerns of the business leader or union leader, then much of what he comes up with is of only very limited immediate use to the practitioner.

The Job of the Social Scientist

This has been only a sketchy review of a few of the better studies of human relations in the workplace. But I think it can tell us something of the respective roles of the social scientist and the practitioner. One reason for the limited here-and-now payoff of social research is that the social scientist's job is basically different from the executive's job. Insofar as he is a social scientist and not a social engineer, the researcher is in the business of building conceptual schemes and testing hypotheses derived from them. To do this he has to abstract from the confusing reality out there, consider only a few things at a time, and imagine that other factors are constant—on the assumption that other factors are less important. He has also to specify the conditions under which his generalizations hold. (He cannot simultaneously believe both that "birds of a feather flock together" and that "opposites attract," using whatever bit of common sense seems convenient at the moment.)

This explains in part why some of the most practical generalizations in the literature I have mentioned may lack any immediate relevance. We tell the leader of an organization that a democratic leadership style along with membership participation in managerial decisions will probably improve organizational effectiveness—i.e., *if* the culture has supplied the members of the work group with an equalitarian ideology, *if* the labor and product market situation

---

and high productivity can flourish: (1) clearly-defined and simple goals; (2) clear-cut division of labor; (3) necessary skills well-known and possessed by group; (4) strong pressures from outside the group itself toward conformity—threat of unemployment, recognized danger to survival (e.g., war, pending bankruptcy of company, etc.). The conditions under which authoritarian leadership might be as effective as its alternatives might include in addition to those above: (1) group members see speedy action as necessary (e.g., urgent task in crisis situation); (2) previous group experience (in family, cliques, work-groups, formal associations, etc.)—sometimes called "the personality factor"—has accustomed group members to authoritarian leadership. It is noteworthy that in the original Lewin *et al.* experiments, the boy from a military family performed "worse" in the group with "democratic" leadership.

has not coerced the members into all-out effort already, *if* the skills of participation are available and the cost not too high, *if* the decision does not necessitate secrecy, *if* major threats from the outside do not necessitate speed, *if* the tasks at hand are varied, require skilled workers, are not clear-cut, simple, and exacting (which probably eliminates two-thirds of the jobs in the American economy), etc. The practitioner must consider all of these possibilities and more; the social scientist takes a few at a time, tries to clarify them, relate them, and establish a firm proposition about them, tested in many situations (so he doesn't end up with what is unique to one). This is time-consuming and costly and very likely will not yield much concrete satisfaction to the practitioner, at least in the short run.

In short, there is for the scientist the necessity of being theoretical; he has to concern himself with basic variables in human conduct—those few facts about life which are recurrent and general. The practitioner, on the other hand, has to consider a given organization at a given place and time with its unique history, traditions, and personalities.

Now this is not to say that a social scientist who temporarily becomes a social engineer cannot exploit his data-gathering position to do a little pure science on the side. A man who consults with industry or labor and applies what little knowledge there is to a practical problem can indeed play simultaneously the role of social scientist. But this involves more than changing the language and sending his report to a different journal. It means he has to be clear about the different purposes of his effort and about the standards of success appropriate to each (a contribution to the solution of the practical problem may involve neither a contribution to knowledge nor the approval of scientific colleagues). Keeping the roles separate may even mean gathering data to serve the scientific interest which would be considered irrelevant to the practical problem.

Neither is this to say that the best theory may not ultimately be the best practice. It may be. The social scientist and practitioner, after all, use the same thought processes and they often have to act without knowing the consequences. Science is both rational and empirical—it uses some system of logic and applies it to data available to the human senses. The practitioner, too, must be rational and empirical. And both scientist and practitioner have to make guesses about how things are related. Bad guesses may be costly in both cases and both may think their errors obvious in retrospect.

But the scientist has to be more self-conscious and deliberate about being rational and empirical. And he can afford more often to be wrong. In fact, he tries continually to prove himself wrong (or at least show that his colleagues are wrong). He has more time for all of this (or should have).

The task for social scientists at this stage of the game, it seems to me, is not to pile up *ad hoc* generalizations and rush to apply them in training programs and personnel philosophies. This is a bit premature. At this stage of social science development we need instead to describe more clearly the variables we consider crucial in human conduct, and we need to digest more carefully and critically the empirical studies done thus far. We run the risk of overselling what social science has to offer the leaders of any interest group. Such overselling can invite both a deserved revulsion for any objective study of man and a sharp withdrawal of tolerance for the university independence which is essential for such study.

Which brings me to a second point about the relation of social scientist to practitioner: many questions of both social and theoretical import may or may not interest the leaders of the groups we study. Questions about change, for instance. Under what conditions do enterprising and innovating ideologies and leadership groups arise and destroy established organizational or social routines? In different types of organizations, what are the points of tension which make for changes in organizational structure? How does succession of leadership in relatively stable organizations take place? How does it affect organizational structure? What variables affect the degree of bureaucratization of an organization? Under what conditions is a process of bureaucratization slowed or reversed? More generally, how can organizations be shaped better to serve democratic values?

Similarly, when human relations researchers tackle trade unions, they might well ask some questions like these in an effort to appraise the union impact on person and society: What kinds of participation do unions open to their members (an old and still a good question)? More important, which of these forms of participation is likely to

(1) further or lessen the worker's identification with the goals and institutions (and definitions of legitimate means) of the larger society; (2) loosen or tighten the member's attachment to family, friendship cliques, and other primary groups; (3) make the member more, or less, susceptible to propagandistic manipulation? Do unions broaden workers' participation in the life of the larger society, or do union activities merely attract those already participating? What is the relation between union involvement and general associational participation? Many people in modern society have multiple and sometimes conflicting group loyalties. Are these people more, or less, susceptible to easy mobilization by the demagogue? In other words, what forms of participation in voluntary associations block the totalitarian potential? Which help to nourish it? Such studies would be useful both for sociological theories of the mass society and for an understanding of the trade union impact.

We need in both the management and the union case a critical look at the quality and varieties of "participation," and, more broadly, at the anti-apathy crusade that has gained momentum in recent years. The big question of how people can be mobilized to pursue common goals without being driven (i.e., coerced) or deceived (i.e., manipulated) is still worth exploring. And the bigger question of how we can structure areas of life where people are simply left to their own devices, to their own autonomous apathy, is even more crucial.

Answers to some of these questions might not interest—and surely would not help—the leaders of the relevant pressure groups; they are not thereby less worth studying.[17]

[17] Some progress is already being made along these lines in studies of a great variety of groups and organizations in many cultural settings. The work of Harbison, Kerr, Myers, and Dunlop on the labor problem in economic development and cultural change; Moore and Simon's studies of organizational behavior at Princeton and Carnegie Tech; Hoselitz, Wohl, and others at Chicago in the Research Center in Economic Development and Cultural Change; the work of Walker and Guest and Kornhauser on social psychological effects of routine work seen in an organizational and community setting; L. Sayles and G. Strauss, *The Local Union: Its Place in the Industrial Plant* (New York: Harper, 1953) and the forthcoming study of the American worker as a union member by the J. Seidman group at Chicago; case studies like A. Gouldner, *Patterns of Industrial Bureaucracy* (Glencoe, Ill.: Free Press, 1954)—all these promise a fruitful attack on the sort of questions raised above. We also have good leads for studies of participation by subordinates in organizational decision-making and the

VALUES AND SOCIAL RESEARCH

The values of the researcher obviously affect his choice of problems and sometimes his perception of the "facts." Mayo's critics have documented this point well. But I think their criticisms need some modification in the light of what the more recent generation of social researchers are doing.

It seems to me that there are two images of the ideal worker which now have a grip on us. These ideal images have guided much of the research since Mayo.

There is first the happy, contented, but autonomous, decision-making, participating worker. He goes about his work with a cheerful willingness to comply with managerial directives, and where management considers it appropriate he participates in decisions, usually of minor importance (but sometimes of major importance) affecting the work situation. This is an image held by many social researchers. It is a reflection of that anti-apathy crusade I spoke of. Sometimes it is rooted in a genuine commitment to democratic values, sometimes not. Sometimes the analysis of the authority structure of the workplace (implied by the image) includes trade unions, sometimes not.

The second image of the ideal worker sees him as happy, contented, but typically docile. He, too, goes about his work with a cheerful willingness to comply with managerial directives. Sometimes, but not too frequently, he exercises limited initiative in the pursuit of managerial aims. He has ambition, but it is ambition with limited goals, compatible with management's requirements that there be discipline, regularity, and somebody to do the less interesting work.[18] Among the managers, company staff experts, and re-

---

problem of apathy in D. Riesman and N. Glazer, "Criteria for Political Apathy," in *Studies in Leadership*, A. Gouldner, ed. (New York: Harper, 1950), pp. 505-559; P. Selznick, *The Organizational Weapon: A Study of Bolshevik Strategy and Tactics* (New York: McGraw-Hill, 1952); and R. Tannenbaum and F. Massarik, "Participation by Subordinates in the Managerial Decision-Making Process," *The Canadian Journal of Economics and Political Science*, XVI (August 1950), pp. 408-418, Reprint No. 14, University of California at Los Angeles.

[18] Cf. George W. Brooks' stimulating remarks on the broad question, "How many individualistic rate-busters can industry stand?" "Labor and Individual Initiative," in *Individual Initiative in Business*, G. H. Allen, ed. (Cambridge: Harvard University Press, 1950), pp. 131-135.

searchers who hold to this second image there is an awful abuse of the English language. "Two-way communication" in this new lexicon means that orders go down, information comes up. "Morale" means "worker satisfaction" which means satisfaction with company attitude and action. "Harmony," as C. W. Mills suggests, is a euphemism for "cheerful willingness to comply with management directives." "Democratic leadership" is translated, "Be a nice guy, be human. Be a good listener. Don't be a boss. Give them the idea they're making the decision, not you." And "human relations" is now defined—I quote a training manual—as "the art of dealing with people in such a manner that they will want to conduct themselves in a desired fashion."[19] I am reminded of the sociologist's image of the perfectly "integrated" society where everyone does what he *has* to do because he *wants* to do it!

Many writers have seen this language and the mentality it suggests as adding up to a society in which manipulation is the chief form of control—manipulation defined as a means of control in which subordinates are unaware of the goals toward which their activity is directed.

Years ago I was worried about this *1984* possibility, too. It was not so much that sociologists and psychologists were selling out to the interests—that they had a managerial bias, were pro-business as opposed to being pro-labor. It was instead the fear that we might develop a society in which the leaders of *all* associations, public or private, are equally adept at manipulating the masses, all acquainted with the leadership style labeled democratic. Since I have met some of the conspirators in this plot and watched them in action, I am somewhat less worried. Those of us who cherish democratic beliefs and want to maximize persuasion and reason in man's affairs have little to fear. Those who prefer the coercive ways of the totalitarian state also have little to fear.

First, while we may be in David Riesman's era of the glad hand, more and more people are catching on to the fact. "Participation" that means nothing more than ritual affirmation of settled policy, "democratic leadership" that means nothing more than a set of charm school gimmicks—these are likely to be less and less effec-

[19] Metropolitan Life Insurance Company, "Training Supervisors in Human Relations" (Report prepared for Metropolitan Group Policy-Holders, 1946).

tive as time goes on. I understand that children in up-to-date orphanages run by well-trained social workers often use the phrase, "You're trying to psychology me!" There is no reason to suppose that a mature worker who sees a studiously calculated "warm smile" on the face of his foreman fresh from a human relations training session will be any less suspicious. Even in the totalitarian state there are some hints that people develop propaganditis.[20] In a free society, healthy skepticism is all the more likely to flourish.

Where democratic participation or democratic leadership styles are more than mere form, the substance they contain is likely to take the form of union organization—a share in control through collective bargaining representatives; or it is likely to create more disturbance and cost than most companies are willing to put up with. At least two of the style-of-leadership studies—one in an insurance company, one in a utility company—offer suggestive data along this line. The first notes that general (v. close) supervision tends to increase employees' aspirations; but if the supervisor cannot deliver and the employee is powerless, it makes for more dissatisfaction.[21] The same in the utility company: supervisors who "sided with the employees" and were "socially close" but who could not deliver "actual benefits" did not increase satisfaction and may have created dissatisfaction.[22]

In a third study—an extraordinarily imaginative and ambitious attempt to carry out a contrived experiment in a large organization—the researchers tried to bring about a major diffusion of authority in one segment of the organization, greater centralization in another, to watch the impact on organizational effectiveness. In some degree they succeeded, despite considerable opposition from many managers. At first the workers in the "autonomous" group were "confused and incredulous," we are told. But they soon began to make decisions—decisions on length of recess, lunch periods, on work assignments and methods. Management was "pleasantly surprised by the modest character of the early decisions." But as the workers "be-

[20] E.g., see Alex Inkeles' analysis of the problems encountered by the Bolshevik "agitator" in the U.S.S.R. *Public Opinion in Soviet Russia* (Cambridge: Harvard University Press, 1950), especially pp. 77 ff.

[21] Morse, *op. cit.*, pp. 124, 141-145.

[22] D. C. Pelz, "Influence: A Key to Effective Leadership in the First-Line Supervision," *Personnel*, XXVIII (November 1952), pp. 215-216.

came more accustomed to their new role, some of the groups began discussing promotion policy, rates of pay and returns to themselves from savings achieved through staff reduction." Management decided to go no further with the delegation of its authority, and the "curve of [worker] decisions soon reached a peak and began to decline."[23]

This experiment reminds me of two features of recent American history and a current feature of British history. The great American steel companies in the 1930's tried once to make modest delegations of authority to employees—in this instance through company unions. It merely served to whet the appetites of the employee representatives who, upon discovering that wages, discipline, promotions, and similar problems were off the bounds of their proper participation, turned their company unions into locals of the CIO Steelworkers. And again in the 1940's the Labor-Management Production Committees fostered by the War Production Board were supposed to stay out of bargaining areas. But to make them effective, deSchweinitz reports, "it was found necessary to have the authoritative representatives of the workers [union officials] as well as of management."[24]

Finally, in Britain today I understand that the ambitious program of joint consultation has encountered similar difficulties. Especially on the productivity-efficiency side and especially outside the government departments, these programs are apparently rather ineffective—despite much exhortation.[25]

[23] E. Reimer, "Creating Experimental Social Change in an Ongoing Organization." Presented at the American Psychological Association meetings, New York, September 1954.

[24] D. deSchweinitz, *Labor and Management in a Common Enterprise* (Cambridge: Harvard University Press, 1949), p. 120.

[25] See Scott, *op. cit.*, especially pp. 72-75, 126-127; National Institute of Industrial Psychology, *Joint Consultation in British Industry* (London: Staples Press, 1952), an interview-questionnaire survey sponsored by the Human Factors Panel of the Committee on Industrial Productivity; and Viteles, *op. cit.*, pp. 460-472. L. R. Tripp offers some uncommon good sense on the worker participation question in America. 'The Union's Role in Industry—Its Extent and Limits," in *Interpreting the Labor Movement* (Madison: Industrial Relations Research Association, 1952), especially pp. 96 ff., 102-109. Cf. Hugh A. Clegg's concise and perceptive analysis of the problem in nationalized industries in Britain. *Industrial Democracy and Nationalization* (Oxford: Blackwell, 1951). Both are bothered by the tendency to obliterate the necessary distinction between the trade union as "watchdog"—protector and aggressive agent re job problems—and management as the "initiating, directing, driving force in an economy."

What all this suggests is that where the administrative necessities (including the maintenance of authority) conflict with the permissive-democratic ideology, the latter tends to give way. Because final responsibility for enterprise welfare is legally and morally in their hands, managers will typically retain final authority to make policy affecting that welfare—whether their style in the exercise of their authority be permissive or autocratic. In a free society this authority will be checked and challenged, policed and criticized by other independent associations and organizations—among them trade unions. Maybe this is why most managers in America hold to neither the cheerful-participating image of the ideal worker nor to the cheerful-docile one. These managers remain untouched by the Human Relations Movement in its democratic *or* pseudodemocratic forms. They do not (like some of their colleagues more affected by the equalitarian strain in American culture) feel guilty when they have to issue an order. They want workers who will produce and obey, within traditional reason, and generally give as little trouble as possible. They are realistic enough to know that trouble there will be, and discontent, too. So long as we allow freedom of association, so long as we remain committed to the notion that power should be both diffused and visible, there will be many independent centers of power and much expression of disharmony. We should be glad of it.

ENVIRONMENT AND TIME PERSPECTIVE

In much of the discussion thus far, I have suggested that many factors outside the workplace, some beyond the control of the manager, shape work conduct and the pattern of social relations inside the workplace. What are these environmental factors?

Much of the human relations research has shown little sensitivity to the environment. It conceives of the workplace as a self-contained social system. There is an obvious necessity of abstraction in social science, and "social system" is one such useful abstraction. But the social system under study must be described with the use of concepts which assure the investigator's awareness of the outer environment at the places where it penetrates and determines the behavior of the system. I will try here only to indicate a line of approach, to give a couple of illustrations and research suggestions.

The factors in the environment that may have some effect on an organization are almost limitless in number. Some of these factors may be extremely important for the fate of an organization but quite irrelevant for social analysis. For instance, a government agency, with its established social structure, traditions and codes, inter-agency relationships, and the like, might be wiped out overnight by a war, a depression, or even by what some Congressional Committee chairman ate for breakfast. The social engineer or practitioner had better keep his eyes on all these possibilities. But the social scientist who wants to do an analysis of patterns of social relations in the agency cannot afford to. He has to look for factors in the environment which are generalizable and recurrent and can be demonstrated to affect organizational behavior. Applied to this case, the research question might be, "What are the typical strategies of adjustment to impending organizational doom?"

Some of the analytically relevant factors in the environment which shape social relations at work are economic and technological —and they take time to take effect. Variations in employment levels, for instance, may cause variations in patterns of impersonality in bureaucracies. When labor and materials are short and demand for the product or service high, maybe the customer or the client gets the brush-off and the job-applicant gets the glad hand, and vice versa.[26] Whether job satisfaction, morale, etc., will be positively or negatively correlated with productivity is also likely to be related to the business cycle. And I am not sure that even now, after a decade of debate about the importance of the economic environment, that my economist friends can tell me the relation of specific economic variables—structure of product market or labor market, elasticity of demand for product, etc.—on the one hand, to the kind and amount of industrial conflict in an industry or firm, on the other. Some of the more enthusiastically interdisciplinary students among us might well focus on this area. A longer time perspective and a sensitivity to the economic environment might lead to the reformulation of some of our propositions about human relations in the workplace.

The second set of analytically relevant environmental variables are social and cultural. Here I can do no more than assert that cul-

[26] Cf. A. Gouldner, "Discussion" of "Industrial Sociology: Status and Prospects," *American Sociological Review*, XIII (August 1948), p. 398.

tural norms and larger social structures *do* penetrate in varying degrees different types of social groups and organizations—and that this is the burden of practically every sociological treatise or textbook that has appeared in recent decades. If you focus on the social conduct of the person in a social position in an organization or even a small group, you are forced to take account of the cultural norms and groups to which he is sensitive. Whether you speak of job satisfaction, morale, the relative importance of economic and noneconomic incentives to work, types of leadership that make for high productivity, or what, you must go beyond the work group, beyond the organization, and into the community and society.

Take the matter of work incentives. If you want to get at the meanings people assign to their work and hence at their likely response to given incentives, you must deal with their group identifications. You need to know the groups whose norms and controls they accept, the groups they take their cues from. This in turn leads to an analysis of the degree to which different groups embrace different cultural values that define the significance of work. Wilbert Moore's excellent analysis of the transformation of peasants into industrial workers in the underdeveloped areas contains hundreds of examples.[27] But we do not have to go to primitive societies in transition to get examples. Studies of the social background of output restricters and rate-busters in our own factories are also relevant.[28] Whether it be a Bemba tribesman who has come to work in a Northern Rhodesia mine and has not yet acquired the appetite for European store-bought clothes, or a Protestant Republican farmer who has come to work in an urban factory and has not yet acquired the taste for output restriction and group loyalty—the worker's cultural background obviously will shape his work conduct.

Or take the problem of the exercise of authority and the response to it. The Ohio State group tells us that popular stereotypes of the leader role derived from the value system of American society is a variable determining actual leader conduct.[29] (An equalitarian strain in the culture dictates that the leader be "one of the boys," not too officious, and that he must avoid making too many demands. But at

[27] W. E. Moore, *Labor and Industrialization* (New York: Cornell University Press, 1951).

[28] Among the best is Collins, Dalton, and Roy, *op. cit.*

[29] See Shartle, Stogdill, and Seeman in Argyris, *op. cit.*, p. 116.

the same time he is supposed to be different, get things done, do things for the group.) Similarly, the studies of Hughes and Merton on professions continually lead them into a consideration of the reciprocal influence of client and professional and a search for the source of the mandate to practice in understanding the conduct of the professional inside the tight inner fraternity. There is always a set of values upholding authority, confirming its legitimacy—whether it be the authority of a professional expert or the authority of a leader in an office. And to get at this you have to move into the society in which the actor acts.

Turn to some of the generalizations in the human-relations-in-industry literature and the point will become clearer. There seem to me to be two related tendencies: (1) a tendency toward psychologizing—i.e., the explanation of a social process in terms of the individual characteristics of the persons involved (personality structure, neurotic predispositions, early childhood training, etc.); and (2) a tendency to study the small group in *vacuo* (ignoring both organizational and cultural environment).

Psychologizing appears in its most extreme form in classic Freudian interpretations of work conduct. Psychiatrist Douglas D. Bond, drawing on years of clinical experience with Air Force fliers in World War II, concludes that the gratification of deep unconscious libidinal and aggressive drives was far more important as a determinant of combat and flying performance than other factors. He notes feminine symbolism in the names of planes ("Violet Virgin," "Messy Bessy," etc.). He observes that "flying has long been known to symbolize sexual intercourse in the unconscious" and love of flying "is not that for another person or object, but rather the narcissistic love for one's own body [the plane]." This ". . . narcissism, the relative indifference to women, and the pronounced rivalry among fliers all point to an unconscious homosexuality"—which explains, too, why they talk about flying so much and why they have such strong solidarity.[30] Similarly, the use of sexual symbolism by workers swearing at their foremen ("they'd stick a knife in you") is seen as a clue to the motivation of a wildcat strike (some men went out on strike to ward off a homosexual attack or an attack on

[30] *Love and Fear of Flying* (New York: International Universities Press, 1952), pp. 140, 146, 22, 25-26.

their manhood).[31] Horseplay in work groups is seen as "regression,"[32] the man operating a drop forge as having strong phallic tendencies, the surgeon as having strong sadistic tendencies, and so on.

For the psychoanalyst, these are entirely proper speculations. It is his task to explain the total psychic life of one individual. He has to consider the projective meaning of the patient's work situation along with everything else. Moreover, there are conditions under which personality variables do have some effect on career patterns and work conduct. For instance, in occupations that allow considerable voluntary self-selection, personality may be important in occupational choices made during the trial and initial stages of a career.[33]

But to take eminently collective phenomena like working class profanity, horseplay, strikes, and explain them on the basis of clinical insight is to miss their basic character. Fliers talk about flying and show strong bonds of solidarity. But any occupational group whose tasks are dangerous and demand great skill talks about the task and displays solidarity toward the lay world (and often factionalism within). So, too, with workers' colorful profanity. It is plausible here to suggest that language usage varies by social class, that industrial workers with the most varied fantasy lives (both in America and in Europe) often use identical designations for their managers. What seems illustrated is not evidence of attacked manhood as a factor in the genesis of a strike, but norms governing the use of profanity. As for horseplay, it is a common form of social control among workers whose work, dress, and status permit it, and need not be explained as infantile regression. And while (to put it loosely) the surgeon may enjoy cutting the patient now as he enjoyed biting the nipple in infancy, his work conduct and career

[31] Gouldner, *Wildcat Strike, op. cit.*, footnote pp. 73-74.

[32] N. R. F. Maier, *Psychology in Industry* (Boston: Houghton Mifflin, 1946), p. 64.

[33] See G. E. Swanson, "Agitation Through the Press: A Study of the Personalities of Publicists," *Public Opinion Quarterly* (forthcoming), one of the few systematic studies of the relation between occupational role and personality. Beginning with an analysis of the role of publicists who specialize in covering controversial issues, Swanson successfully predicted that the personalities of student publicists on the *Michigan Daily* would display strong tendencies of an anal expulsive, phallic, and oral passive sort.

pattern are more likely shaped by relations with his colleagues and clients, the structure of the hospital where he works, popular stereotypes of the occupation, etc., than by oral sadistic tendencies in his personality. In short, it is the main job of the social scientist not to explain the subconscious life of an individual but to establish relationships between extra-individual "social facts."

The tendency to psychologize also accounts for some of the treatment of the small group in *vacuo*. Much of the research and writing focused on the internal dynamics of the small group is preoccupied with such variables as individual needs or job satisfactions, likes and dislikes, degree of attraction or repulsion, frequency of "interaction," and so on. For example, Argyris says, "The informal group . . . is based on need-fulfillment and cohesion imbedded in the members liking each other."[34] Similarly, Homans, in a book of great clarity, tell us that ". . . persons who interact frequently with one another tend to like one another."[35]

Now if links to the environment were taken account of, if the conceptualization were more sociological and less psychological, these generalizations might be much modified. Cohesion or solidarity may have little to do with likes and dislikes, friendship or affection—and frequency of interaction at times has little to do with either cohesion or friendship. There are, for instance, these three common situations: (1) members interact frequently and yet dislike one another (e.g., situations where interaction is imposed by society as in the case of siblings or by organizations as in the case of work crews); (2) members have high *esprit de corps* (that sense of belonging together which is based on personal rapport) and yet do not interact frequently (e.g., scholars, close friends, or lovers apart); and (3) members interact frequently and have high morale (a sense of collective purpose based on common conviction) and yet dislike one another. In all these cases cohesion is likely to be high (whether cohesion is defined as adherence of group members to group norms or as the resultant of all forces acting on the members to remain in the group). Take the third case. High cohesion here is best tested when the group faces adversity—union solidarity in a strike, Army solidarity in battle, church solidarity in time of religious persecution,

[34] Argyris, *op. cit.*, p. 25.
[35] *The Human Group* (New York: Harcourt Brace, 1950), pp. 111-112.

the informal work group in opposition to management, and so on. The members may conform for many varied reasons. They may have many varied motives. They may even represent many different personality types. The important thing is they conform to group norms. In fact the members may hate one another roundly as they carefully conform to common norms and ideologies. Think, for instance, of some of the sectarian political or religious groups you know.

If a member deviates, here again you have to look for a social referent—the multiple identifications of the actor, his adherence to the conflicting norms of some other *outside* group or groups. The research problem here, if you deal with social conduct in groups, is to analyze the extent to which these multiple loyalties and identifications exist, how they are in conflict, how they are reconciled.[36] Put another way, the problem is to study the strategies of adjustment of people caught in the cross-fire of competing claims—whether they be labor or company staff experts concerned about conflicting professional and organizational demands or professors and scientists caught between the conflicting demands of their academic disciplines, on the one hand, and various community groups they feel they should serve, on the other.[37]

This point about relations with environment is important not only in analyzing the internal dynamics of small groups, but also in the treatment of the formal structure of large organizations. An old sociological generalization derived from Sumner goes like this: "Centralized control is maximized in formal organizations when rapid action is regarded as imperative and members feel threatened from outside groups." The important variable here is the degree of conflict with the social environment.

[36] Studies which try to get at this problem include B. Willerman, "Overlapping Group Identification in an Industrial Setting," mimeographed (Ann Arbor: Institute for Social Research, University of Michigan, September, 1949); and Collins, *et al., op. cit.*

[37] See H. L. Wilensky, *Intellectuals in Labor Unions: Organizational Pressures on Professional Roles* (Glencoe, Ill.: Free Press, 1956), in part a study of changes in the role orientations of trade union staff experts. On the professor, see L. Wilson, *The Academic Man* (London: Oxford University Press, 1942); on the research scientist, H. Baumgartel, "An Analysis of Selected Factors in Laboratory Morale," in *Interpersonal Factors in Research* (Ann Arbor: Survey Research Center, University of Michigan, 1954), Chap. 4.

In all of this, of course, the degree to which the larger environment penetrates varies. Pictures of self-contained social systems with little attention to environment may apply pretty well to some groups and organizations, not so well to others. Some groups involve an intimate sharing of thought and feeling by persons in sustained interaction linked in clearly-defined statuses and roles. These groups develop considerable autonomy. They are sometimes impermeable even to the boldest attempts at penetration by a central authority. The Church in Nazi Germany apparently survived a decade of Nazi rule with much of its organizational integrity intact. Perhaps Army High Commands in the modern state have something of this character—judging from the frequency of revolts and the necessity of purges. Perhaps some academic departments in our great universities would fit the description, too.

In contrast, we have more diffuse social structures with statuses and roles that proliferate into the outside and are less clearly defined. These organizations are perhaps best conceived as a set of actors playing (with shifting stance and style) to a varied and shifting set of audiences, only some of which are internal. Some of our national multi-industrial, multicraft trade unions seem to me to be of this character. Some peripheral reform groups like the WCTU (which depends almost wholly on church functionaries and in some places on property-owner associations for its support and membership recruiters) may also fit.[38]

The conceptual problem of drawing boundaries around such organizations and saying, "Here the organization stops, here the environment begins," is a difficult one. In some of these diffuse organizations I get the impression that a large proportion of functionaries are contact men, liaison men of one sort or another—some not even on the payroll. Their contacts cut across formal organizational boundaries and so do their identifications.[39] Perhaps this is a strategic area for research. It might help us clarify the boundaries of different types of organizations and get some picture of the larger structure constituted by their interlinkages.

[38] See J. Gusfield, "Change and Continuity in an Organized Interest Group: A Study of the Woman's Christian Temperance Union" (Doctoral dissertation, University of Chicago, 1954).

[39] Cf. Stogdill who found in a study of submarine personnel (630 enlisted men) that "respondents whose work relationships extend beyond their formal unit tend to err in the direction of perceiving persons with whom they work as members of their own formal chart unit." Quoted in Argyris, *op. cit.*, p. 148.

COMMENTARY ON MR. WILENSKY'S CHAPTER

BY JAMES C. WORTHY
Sears, Roebuck and Company

I wholly agree with Mr. Wilensky that "not everything done by the social scientist can or should help the practitioner." This generalization applies as well to the theoretical physicist in his relation to the engineer as it does to the social scientist in his relation to the administrator. In both cases, the progress of science would be seriously impeded by too much concern about the practical, everyday value of particular lines of inquiry and speculation. I am inclined to think, however, that the work of the social scientist is of greater value to the practitioner than Mr. Wilensky is willing to concede.

Admittedly, there is need to "describe more clearly the variables we consider crucial in human conduct and . . . to digest more carefully and critically the empirical studies done thus far." It nevertheless remains that even in its present tentative and far from perfect state the science of human relations is of considerable value to the practitioner. In the first place, no science is ever complete; it is always in a state of evolving. If we wait for finality, we shall wait forever and deprive ourselves of the value of what we already have. A little knowledge is better than no knowledge and imperfect guidance is better than blind groping.

In the second place, the scientist is not alone in his interest in truth and the pursuit thereof. The practitioner, too, is concerned that his practice be sound. He is anxious to gain a better picture of what his problems are and how he can best come to grips with them. The great interest of businessmen in human relations research is not so much a yearning for gimmicks as a seeking for understanding. And for that purpose, there is real value in exposure to tentative, inconclusive, or even contradictory hypotheses. One of the great services of human relations research is that it has so greatly stimulated the thinking of practical men of affairs.

In addition, many of the specific findings in this field are susceptible of practical application. Consider, for example, the observations cited by Mr. Wilensky regarding the plus and minus values for management of the more closely-knit interpersonal relationships that are characteristic of smaller work groups. He is quite correct in noting that the resulting higher degree of worker solidarity often serves to frustrate the aims of management, but this does not *necessarily* follow. Human relations research, in pointing up the relationship between the size of the work group and the strength of group solidarity puts management on notice that here is an area deserving its attention.

One of the measures of the effectivenes of an organization is the extent to which the aims of the informal organization correspond with those of the formal. Management, by its attitudes and practices, can determine within limits the degree of correspondence that will prevail. Human relations research has suggested some of the general lines along which answers may be found. The Stouffer studies of Army life suggest that strong primary group solidarity can serve to strengthen the large formal organization when, among other things, "there is a predisposing general sense of obligation to the larger purpose of the organization and a readiness to acknowledge the leader's right to command." This proposition throws considerable light on one of the central problems of management.

We cannot dismiss the "larger purpose" of a business enterprise in peacetime as simply making a profit. Certainly that is one of the purposes of any private business enterprise, but it is not the only purpose. The primary purpose of any business enterprise is to produce certain goods or services which contribute in one way or another to the security and well-being of people. Other purposes include provision of the means of livelihood for the members of the organization, provision of opportunity for personal growth and advancement, and provision of an important part of the worker's total way of life. Admittedly, it would be asking a great deal of workers to expect them to be enthusiastic over making bigger profits for absentee stockholders, but it is certainly possible for them to identify with some of these broader purposes.

In emphasizing the importance of "a predisposing general sense of obligation to the larger purpose of the organization," human relations research has not stated a problem beyond the capacity of management to solve. On the contrary, it focuses management's attention on a problem which must be solved and which management alone can solve. This is the proper definition of the purposes of the enterprise and the definition in meaningful terms of the relationship between those purposes and the primary work group.

The manager's problem is not that of "bending the informal work group to the purposes of the enterprise." Rather, it is so conducting the enterprise that the relationship between its purposes and those of the primary work group are clearly apparent. Human relations research has been criticized, sometimes justly, for seeming to imply that all the adjustments to the requirements of modern life should be made by the workers and for providing management with the tools to enforce such adjustments. In another perspective, however, human relations research is calling attention to the changes which managers must make in their conceptions of their own responsibilities and in their own manner of behavior.

I share Mr. Wilensky's confidence that we are not headed for an Orwellian society "in which manipulation is the chief form of control." I agree with him that gimmicks and devices employed for purposes of manipulation will soon lose their effectiveness. The important question is management's motives in employing the results of human relations research. If its motives are those of narrow self interest, of finding subtler and smoother ways of bending workers to its will, the effort will be worse than useless for it will widen further the gap between workers and management. But if management's motives are sincerely those of better understanding the problems of people at work, of finding ways for making work a more rewarding experience, of discovering its own shortcomings and means for improvement, management's efforts to apply the findings of human relations research are likely to create positive benefits for all concerned.

Much human relations research has been highly creative. By no means all of it is immediately useful to the practitioner, and that is as it should be. But the practitioners are interested, perhaps to an extent that scientists laboring in the field fail to appreciate.

Human relations research has already made important contributions to the preservation of traditional values in face of the stresses and strains of modern urban-industrial life. These contributions will undoubtedly continue to grow, perhaps at an accelerated tempo.

The scientists may be confident that the practitioner will make frequent and fruitful use of their findings. The scientists may be confident, too, that by and large these findings will be used with integrity and as a means of strengthening, not undermining, the traditional values of our American democratic society.

PART II

THE URBAN-INDUSTRIAL SETTING: HUMAN RELATIONS IN CONTEXT

· IV ·

WORK AND THE CHANGING AMERICAN SCENE

BY CONRAD M. ARENSBERG
Columbia University

A book on recent research and practical interest in the human relations of people at work requires that the subject be put in perspective. It has a long history, which began with the original protest against the machine, and has come down to us through recent decades of progress toward an empirical social and psychological science. It has always embodied a realistic concern with understanding adjustments among the human beings who occupy the many positions required by the immense and growing complexity of the organization by which our civilization produces and distributes its goods. It has often as well embodied some sort of hope for an ameliorative redirection of these adjustments. The purpose of the improvement is and has been various: humanitarian, manipulative, interested, partisan. In general the subject matter has defined the field, not the purpose, despite recurrent criticisms inspired by worries about the end to which the slowly-won knowledge of human relations and their effects at work might be put.

Certainly the world's work today calls for less brawn and handicraft and more brain, patience, good temper—things that make up precisely the ability to plan for and live with intricate organizations of human beings. "Human relations" research, like organization theory—another branch of man's attempts at rational self-understanding and self-management—ultimately treats the conditions of incentive, emotion, and acceptance which make cooperation in such organization possible at all. In so doing it cannot be merely a device for the better milking of contented cows, as some critics have called it. Most broadly seen, it must grow instead into a necessity for survival, both institutional and general. More narrowly seen, as in these pages, it is merely that aspect of our modern efforts at self-understanding and rational self-direction, or our efforts at self-blandishment, that rests on observation of and concern with the world of workshops, factories, and business or administrative offices. It is the local branch of our modern social science—from laboratory experiment about human beings in interaction to perhaps premature application—which is at home with the men, the machines, the rule-books, and the sentiments inhabiting that theater of modern life. If it has all the troubles of modern social science—difficulties of winning objectivity, of definition, of finding bases for prediction, of separating factors in complexities, of treating human beings as objects of science—these same troubles beset modern man everywhere in his effort to swing the powerful searchlights of his science upon himself. If it has special troubles, seizure by overeager devotees, manipulators and Machiavellians, or political partisans, or too-narrow concern with the workshop alone, that is because its theater—our work life—is a difficult, fast-changing, and highly sensitive part of our lives, about which no one is neutral long.

Other chapters will spell out the concerns of scientist, businessman, unionist, and moral and social commentator which have played their parts in what the Bendix chapter has shown to have developed as "human relations" theory and practice in the industrial setting. Before we can begin such specifications, however, it is well to put the whole matter in the larger framework of the place in modern America of the industrial theater itself. There have been, and still are, major technological, cultural, and social trends in present-day American civilization which directly affect human beings and their relations at work. Some may make for a latter-day climate in which older notions are no longer adequate and newer ones, critical, self-appraising, or self-congratulatory, are welcome. While it is manifestly impossible for Americans, or anyone, in mid-course of change and in midstream of movement, to understand completely the currents which carry them onward, it may well be useful to try a summation of these trends as they impinge upon the work America does and the lives of the people who do it.

Neither the nature of the jobs most people at work perform nor the nature of the people themselves apart from their work are any longer very much as we used to be accustomed to see them. Let us take stock of some dominant changes in these things, at least as they compare with our received ideas about them.

NATURE OF THE JOBS

First, the jobs modern Americans do are not those of the independent, self-sufficient, small farmer, the pioneer, yeoman, or rugged individualist of the country's founding and expansion. Some subsistence farmers survive, but often the farmer today is a master of machines and planner of production for sale, more and more like his industrial counterpart, or he is himself employee of the "factory in the field." Nor are the jobs of the independent businessmen any longer representative, though a few industries and a few new specialty lines, in the tertiary industries, still keep alive the tradition of personalized, individual business leadership and successful small-scale operation. The smaller businessman and the independent shopkeeper, self-employed and self-directing, survive in smaller cities, suburbs, and older urban residential wards, as do closed family-owned and managed enterprises on the nineteenth-century model still widespread in Europe. But they are fewer each year and less pace-setting, just as each year they employ fewer workers from the great mass of the population.

Both in production and in distribution today the modern American is an employee, whether managerial, white-collar, blue-collar, of a large corporation. Business is corporate business, both in the substantially correct modern public image and in its function of setting prices, policies, and employment conditions.

But that is not all: the corporate establishments in which the modern American works are not only big, they are growing bigger, older, and more deeply established, diversified as to their bases in products produced or distributed, their resources owned, managed, planned for. Furthermore, they are more and more multiplant corporations, with branches and offices and factories in many metropolitan cities, in remaining mill towns, in new suburban and raw-countryside plants. If he has a blue collar, the employee is likely also to be a member of an equally large and sprawling union, of which his local and branch are one of many covering the same spread of common interests his corporation covers. If he is a manager or white collar, he is no longer responsible to a personal captain, but to a corps of committeemen and boards in an increasingly elaborate and professionalized hierarchy of career-dedicated corporate businessmen. For both of them, the company is a lifelong civil service, with a company or union pension and retirement plan beckoning at the end of a long and seniority-building career. At the top of the ladder of positions movement must be slow, open to only a few, or not possible at all for most.

For the blue-collar and perhaps increasingly for the white-collar, the paycheck and its fringes and an early retirement into tertiary or independent employment or leisure, rather than advancement and accomplishment on the job, seem to be the goal of work. Perhaps it is only the manager who, company-minded but professionally alert as well, can push himself up into the lofty horizons of "big success," coming to direct, control, even manipulate these increasing corporate hierarchies. It is natural that Americans of all stripes and positions in this new world of career-business and organization work should try to rethink the motivations and the human relationships which unite or divide them as they follow these careers. They have done so not only in regard to the large-scale industrial relations of workers v. managers and company v. union but also in the small scale of in-plant life, where worker and worker, manager, foreman, shop steward, and worker, engineer and clerk and machine-tender, all come together or pass one another by. Our interest in such "human relations" is expectable when we review these new conditions.

Thus, the careers of most people at work have changed out of recognition, away from the traditional views we once had of them. It is equally true that the actual work Americans perform on the job is very different from what it used to be. Increased scale of organization meant decreased autonomous control over one's own work life, tools, and skills. The growth of planning in production and distribution, the growth of controls and checks and audits of performance, the reduction of skills to blueprinted minutiae of labor and effort, coordinated and timed into simultaneous manufactures flowing to final assemblies, have long ago spread from the workbench of the blue-collar upward and outward to the engineer's drafting room, the clerk's counting house and file room, the grocer's supermarket, or the wholesaler's warehouse. American knowhow is not so much the knowhow of science and skill, it is rather the knowhow of organization, coordination, teamwork, and planning, the application of theories and discoveries to large-scale execution.

Thus the "human relations" interest which began with a humanist protest against the Machine may soon find itself landed in a paradoxical spot. For the single machine is no longer the center of our modern American's work. He is no longer typically the machine-tender, the robot dancing attendance on the mechanical monster of Charlie Chaplin's "Modern Time." Ironically, we finally know a great deal about the men and women feeding the machines of the Western Electric Company's Relay Assembly Test Room, for example, or about the irksome disciplines of the impersonally moving assembly line, at the very moment in our technological and industrial engineering development when automation "technologically displaces" the machine-tender himself.

"Automation" is a word much discussed and little understood today, but some things about it are clear. The "flow of work" in the assembly line, or between one machine and the next, and the coordination of pace and precision which substituted the repetitious, standardizing machine for the human hand and eye, are now being built into the plant and machines and control of the factory itself. In this sense we are achieving "automatic production" in one industry after the other, and the machine-tender will be free. He may, as is already the case in oils and chemicals, become dial-watcher, chart-reader, and "stationary engineer." But his job need never bind him to small moving parts in one spot and to the old monotony and fixity which made him over the years an "interchangeable hand" tending an "interchangeable machine" making "interchangeable parts" against the stopwatch and the moving-line of the coordinating manager-engineer.

Naturally, it will be a long time before the "automative" millennium will come to every American business, and it may never come.

Human relations of the tended machine and the moving line will continue to occupy us theoretically and practically. But already management and union, as well as the commentators among us from social science, morality, and politics, have such new relations to worry about. What are the skills and responsibilities of the dial-watchers? How shall they be recompensed and motivated and yet kept under control by the planners and financers of the new automatic processes? Few seem yet to be addressing themselves to these matters, although they concern the eventual survivors of this new "second industrial revolution." Labor and the public, of course, as they did long ago in the first one, are worrying about what will become of the displaced and how the new factories shall be manned. But later on they, too, perhaps, will need to think about the "in-plant human relations" of the new automative plants just as they have thought and agitated about these things in the more familiar factories of the present and recent past.

One old worry will certainly carry over. Much has been said and written about the fate of the craftmanship, inventiveness, and workmanship which American industry inherited from the long tradition of European artisanry and which American genius built into the huge proliferations of modern industrial "knowhow." The theme will continue to be central to much speculation about our age, just as it has been basic to research in "human relations." If standardization, necessary for the precision which made parts interchangeable for final assemblies, substituted machines for such skills and trivialized work, it also turned the worker from a man who produced things to one who produced units. The machine-tender came to be measured not for his accomplishment but for his output score. He no longer controlled, planned, serviced, or even paced his own work or the machine that made his scores; others in the organization employing him, disciplining him, scoring and paying him for those units did those things. We already know a great deal of the consequences of this long drawn-out change in bench work, in the century-long study of the "problems of labor unrest." Human relations research has continued to observe and explore these problems and what can be done about them. But that same original inventiveness, stripped from the worker by the growth of industrial organization, seems not to have disappeared, as Veblen once feared.

Instead, that inventiveness seems only to have left the workroom for the drawing-board or for the worker's participation in resistance to management, in union activity, in recreation, etc. The engineer built it into the very machines which nowadays rationalize away the remaining trivial jobs, until finally, with automation, even the assembly-line itself may disappear and continuous mechanical flow from machine to machine takes its place. And despite all personnel plans from incentive schemes through suggestion boxes to the Scanlon Plan, that inventiveness seems to have left the workroom without leaving the worker himself. Perhaps when the engineers functionalized the original "Yankee ingenuity" out of the shop, the worker merely took his share of it home with him.

Much is being written today, like our chapter on "Leisure" in this book, that gives rise to the suspicion that American inventiveness has not gone down before industrialization. The new social skills of management, the new-won rights of unionism, the incentives to output in money earned for boom-time consumption goods and life benefits, seem not to be so much substitutes for the worker's loss of pride, control, and motive in "his instinct of workmanship," as they seem to be responses to a division of labor. The instinct of workmanship flourishes now, we are told, in leisure. It flowers in the endless do-it-yourself work, the care of cars and hobbies and machine-toys, the inventive puttering of life after work. Inventiveness, once a part of every artisan's work, has become instead the career job of the technician and the research man. The loss for work democracy, and even work interest, is clear; no one denies it. And the student of "human relations" must deal with it quite consciously, either piecemeal in plans for personnel palliatives, or organically, in contriving other "group dynamics" in the organization of today's work procedures and disciplines. In the same way, the union, if it operates within the living "business unionism" of our society, must first push grievances arising from the present reality rather than plan for an industrial order which puts the worker in another role than modern worker. "Human relations" research is not the design for social orders, or the comparison of civilizations. It is and has been the exploration of the fate of human beings in the world inherited by our age, including those caught in the sacrifices exacted by a brilliant cooperative technology like ours.

That displacement of inventiveness from the workroom to the research laboratory and the design board, from worker to scientist and technician, and from working hours in the shop to leisure at home or after retirement, is an ironical end, perhaps, to one of the great old problems of human relations at work: The Problem of Man and the Machine with which it all began. The promise of the next advance in our industrial organization is that the worker, no longer tender, becomes driver of the intricate machines that set up, pace, do, assemble, and score the work, both of factory and of office. Much evolution will have to take place before this new role is perfected. The issue is already joined in industrial relations. The "nonproduction workers" in machine-watching, maintenance, and direction have come in many industries to be more numerous than the "production workers," that old category of those who turn out directly the particular units of each machine station in manufacture. How shall they be controlled, timed, paced, scored, paid? They do not turn out units any longer; instead they are responsible for flows, for smooth functionings, for coordinations of machine-operations, for costly and delicate installations. Once again they exercise judgment, make decisions, set pace or condition in the process that produces the thing. We have few studies here and little experience from which to guess. But human relations research must learn to watch this evolution, too, as it has tried to watch those of the machine in the past. And both manager and unionist will need help, like the citizen and the worker, in recasting old definitions and old conventions to suit the new reality. The new automation may not have turned the worker into a new skilled master and driver-pilot of his machines. But the promise is already here.

NATURE OF PEOPLE APART FROM WORK

But what of the trends outside work itself? If the kind of work we do is changing out of recognition, if old drudgeries, replacing the remaining crafts, disappear with the spread of machines, of new paper skills, and of new intricate teamwork patterns from production into white-collar and managerial functions themselves, what of future human relations?

Certainly trends outside work are bringing about a new American civilization with many features which cannot fail to affect us in our work and in our industrial relations. The critics of human relations research, as we shall see in the chapters of this book, have always insisted that behavior and sentiment in industry reflect conditions and currents from the economy and the society at large. Their insistence must guide us in the future.

It seems clear that, no less than at work, we are facing an upgrading of labor outside in the community. This is more than a local instance of the world-wide "leveling" of class and income differentials, a disappearance of the distinctions between white collar and blue. Current high levels of employment, high incomes, repeated annual improvements in status and benefits, narrow or reverse the old income gap. The spread of home ownership, the entrance of the workers into the suburbanization of our cities, the generalization of consumption standards through installment buying and other extensions of credit are wiping away visible differences.

But it is not yet clear whether these new conditions are fully homogenizing inner attitudes. If culture today is "mass culture," and the metropolitan market continues to grow, workers certainly share in it, some of them better than some former middle-class groups. Especially significant is the continuing decline of racial, religious, and nationality discrimination, both in industrial jobs and to an important extent in community life. While barriers to social interaction still remain or fade more slowly, those once hedging opportunities for occupational mobility and public institutional participation are falling very fast. And the blue-collars stand to benefit. The path of upward social mobility and the chance to relinquish forced membership in closed groups, ethnic or regional, continue to lie open to Americans and to beckon more and more of them. Such growing freedom for the individual to make his own group-memberships, deepening the "voluntarism" which has long marked American life on so many institutional fronts, cannot help but influence human relations at industry. We know already that it has made many changes in the tone and manner of public life and of office and shop practice, both in helping drive underground the former overt ethnic and religious discriminations and discourtesies and in extending to group after group of Americans new and old, white and nonwhite, the possibility of "nicer things," newer quarters, educations for children, influence in our institutions (like the union, or politics). The possibility of realizing such goals outside work, with high pay, at retirement, through savings or installments, cannot fail to have made it more possible for our industry to continue to depersonalize and rationalize work, to substitute the paycheck and the "fringe" for interest in the job, to accept the sacrifices of machine and quota work which we have already mentioned.

Nevertheless, leveling is not necessarily standardization. As with the "Yankee" instinct of workmanship, the many and culturally diverse aspirations of the ethnic groups of our complex civilization did not need to leave the persons of the workers. The workers' diverse cultural heritages could merely leave the workshop and go home with them after hours.

Thus it would be a mistake to misread the substantial victories of "cultural pluralism" and decent intergroup relations in recent American life. There is an undeniable leveling of consumption standards going on, as a growth in the standardization and "regimentation" of a public "mass culture." The fear of those who have protested The Machine, on artistic and humanitarian grounds as well as on political ones, has been from the very beginning that the loss of pride, skill, and self-direction, the robotization at work would deaden permanently the mental and cultural life of the worker. There is much evidence that in early stages of industrialization, during the Great Transformation of Professor Polanyi, that is precisely the effect, when old crafts and interests do die, just as, in early industrialization, harsh and exploitative disciplines, had equally brutalizing effects. But a mellowing and evolving industrialization, whether or not the students of industrial and human relations have helped, seems perhaps to be in process of making its own peace with culture and society outside the factory and to be beginning to adapt itself to other institutions: union, mass market, mass leisure, surburban living, social security. In this it may prove itself capable of rounding out a civilization more humane, more full in its own way (whether we like the way or not), and better articulated upon itself. It should come as no surprise, then, to learn that the worker, caught like all of us in the new metropolitan life burgeoning outside his place of employ, has more and newer things to choose from, new and more varied goals to turn his mind to, off the job.

Off the job, the worker's goals are by no means the goals of the mass market alone. There are also goals, postponed at work, which stick to a man, even if unconsciously, from his cultural heritage. In a world where, as today, more and more of our work is done by one age class alone—the men and women, substantially, between twenty and fifty—the short span of industrial work-years is not enough to drown that heritage. The shorter hours on the job, or jobs performed not for their interest but for their take-home pay, leave energy for after-hours plans. At any rate in the East, if less so perhaps in the newer industrialism of Middle West and South, the Italian worker from the south Italian mountain village, with a tradition of retirement in a family in which a younger person can take over earning, can think of leaving the job for a small house and vineyard patch in the "rurban fringe," where his unmarried sons or daughters can find jobs in the new factories and specialty shops going up in the former potato fields. The mill-working American French Canadian or Pole can buy up the abandoned Yankee farm (if the summer people don't get it first), and his children keep on in the new plastics or specialties firms in the abandoned mill buildings of the lost textile industry. The Jewish garment-worker, his "lerner" son triumphantly supported through college and into the new American version of the traditional trade movement, can hope for a candy-store. The levelings and the metropolitanization of modern American life are insistent and compelling as they keep pace with the endless proliferation of rationalization and "knowhow" inside the industrial plant, but we need not fear that they dissolve the old traditions entirely. The richly diverse social and cultural heritages of the country, our unconscious and often unacknowledged counterpoise to the sweeping integration of the dominant and dynamic technical, economic, and political institutions of our civilization, seem in little danger of disappearing. Even with common use of English and the fading out of the original immigrant colonies, the American ethnic groups, both those of the "majority" stocks like Texans, Mormons, Yankees, and other regional Old Descendants, and those of the "minority ones" of the "nationalities" and the races we still recognize as separate traditions, are not breaking up. Instead, the sociologists tell us, they are consolidating and working for equal recognition. These heritages may well supply the more and more diverse goals for which paychecks and incentive bonuses mount up. The role of the great mass markets, in the growing metropolitan cities which provide a mosaic of suburbs, urban wards, satellite cities, and residential housing developments, where peer group contacts with neighbors are balanced with remembered ties to relatives and ethnic fellows, is to make all the diverse aspirations of cultural tradition legitimate, respectable, and possible. To level is not necessarily to standardize, especially in the mixed tastes of the life after hours where the pay envelope is put to use. And to displace interest, purpose, and inventiveness from the job and from the workshop, when one can take it home or expend it in human and industrial relations, is not necessarily to lose it from American life and from the lives of those who work.

· V ·

WORK AND LEISURE: FUSION OR POLARITY?*

BY DAVID RIESMAN AND
WARNER BLOOMBERG, JR.
University of Chicago

As if reflecting the gulf which widened between work and leisure with the rise of the factory, there has been some tendency to regard leisure as not quite a serious topic.[1] Only occasionally does a student of factory life note the consequence of divergent leisure patterns for the forms of industrial relations.[2] We know of nothing for con-

* This is a publication of the Center for the Study of Leisure at the University of Chicago, supported by a grant from the Behavioral Sciences Division of the Ford Foundation.

[1] Thus, while noting that leisure can be a crucial importance, R. F. Tregold (*Human Relations in Modern Industry* [New York: International Universities Press, 1950]), devotes but three pages to it (cf. pp. 70-72), while C. H. Lawshe *et al.* (*Psychology of Industrial Relations* [New York: McGraw-Hill, 1953], pp. 50-53) sees leisure rather narrowly in terms of its effects on productivity. Conversely, many books on leisure (e.g., Martin and Esther Neumeyer, *Leisure and Recreation* [New York: A. S. Barnes, 1947]) make only tangential contact with work as setting the time, energy, and often compensatory nature of play. A greater sense of the dialectic between work and leisure can be found in Foster Rhea Dulles, *America Learns to Play* (New York: D. Appleton-Century, 1940), and notably in Johan Huizinga, *Homo Ludens* (Boston: Beacon Press, 1955).

[2] Thus Alvin Gouldner (*Patterns of Industrial Bureaucracy* [Glencoe, Ill.: Free Press, 1954]) observes that miners and millworkers behave differently among each other and with supervisors and sees these patterns refracted in their behavior off the job. Elton Mayo, of course, devoted passionate attention to the reveries and off-the-job worries which the Hawthorne Plant workers brought from their often underprivileged and under-cosmopolitan homes.

temporary workers comparable to William F. Whyte's *Street Corner Society*—an incredibly conscientious and sensitive "time-study" of the seldom interrupted leisure of the unemployed "corner boys" in a Boston slum. In the present situation, where specialist students of industry and of leisure seldom meet, the broad generalizations of those critics of capitalism for whom both work and leisure are subsumed under such headings as "alienation" become all the more important: for them, work and leisure are alternative names for meaninglessness or exploitation. In an earlier draft, we expatiated on both these and some of the specialist literature, criticizing, comparing, and commending, but since further compression is now asked of us, we have decided to concentrate on our own speculations, fed from these sources, and on our limited personal experiences. The latter (which we don't dignify as "research") are almost entirely confined to the Midwest.

Each of us has argued in earlier writings that (1) leisure must provide meanings and satisfactions, even challenges, which work no longer furnishes for many, both because of changes in the nature of work and in our nature; (2) work and leisure are becoming increasingly indistinct—reminiscent in some ways of the preindustrial age—with interpersonal relations growing in importance in both; (3) factory workers at play are coming increasingly to behave like the general American population, raising the question whether their widely shared roles as consumers (a word we use very broadly to connote nonwork spheres) do not influence their outlook at least as much as their segregated roles as producers. In what follows, we propose to qualify and complicate some of these ideas.

THE CENTRALITY OF WORK

At the beginning of the industrial revolution, Adam Smith was so impressed with the stultifying nature of factory life that he hoped the hours away from work might somehow strengthen those qualities of character he regarded as essentially human. Marx went much further in seeing the factory as the ambush of brutishness, so terrible that it might engender a rational revolt against itself. No doubt, both men overlooked elements of passivity and boredom in the peasant's life, the yeoman's life, to which they could still look back.

Quite possibly, they missed elements of creativity, disguised in tricks of the trade or sabotage or group solidarity, in the factories of their times—though the day was still a long way off when time study departments would assume that two-and-a-half of the eight hours in a steel mill would admittedly be nonproductive, with many workers managing to import into the factory ever larger bits and pieces of their nonwork games and reveries.

Despite such shadings of the bleak picture which has come down to us, it seems fair to generalize that industrialism in England and America came with such speed as to force into the mills people of an essentially rural tradition, unprepared for the shift, so that their merriment became pushed to the fringes of life, hardly more by the arduousness of the factory itself than by the inroads of Puritan uplift. These "fringe benefits" were the remnants of night and Sunday—with the tavern and the church shifting from a village or parish setting to an urban one.[3] They included occasional "seasons" of unemployment, and the increasingly rare holidays (Everett C. Hughes reminds us that in the Catholic Rhineland the first strikes were occasioned by Protestant ironmasters' cutting down the very large number of saints' days and other holidays characteristic of pre-industrial Europe).

Some workers responded to the exhausting demands of the workplace by a heroic effort to build up a counterlife outside the plant —for instance, through the Mechanics' Associations which thrived in mid-nineteenth century America among workers newly introduced to print and the scientific outlook. Some retired into a close-knit family life and to home-improvement rather than self-improvement, here aided by the tradition of "do-it-yourself" carried over from the countryside or from the handicrafter's household and abetted by leakage of factory tools and materials. In the smaller towns and cities, there remained access to hunting and fishing in slack seasons, and gardening one's own or some unclaimed patch of land in the summer—all this regarded more as work to supplement

[3] The L. S. Ayres department store in Indianapolis made the discovery that when it gave its employees Monday off (rather than a shifting weekday) many more went to church Sunday, for they could use the following day to rest up and catch up; undoubtedly, the present phenomenal rise in church attendance among Americans owes a good deal to the shorter work-week and two-day weekend.

the meager earnings rather than as a chosen hobby or relaxation.

Where no other escape existed, the factory workers tended, like sailors, to fall back on the common denominator of the male sex as defining their leisure: gambling, fighting, whoring. This common denominator was especially important because the factory, almost everywhere it appeared, threw together men of different regional and ethnic traditions, and thus made even more difficult the creation of a new and more appropriate urban and industrial pattern of life and leisure. The emerging industrial culture made work central to a man's image of himself, and yet almost entirely separate both from his past and from the meager resources he had left over outside of work. Men became habituated to the factory, as children to school, but this "second nature" never overtook them completely nor turned them into enthusiastic addicts of monotony.

No wonder that a counterattack soon began against the central place of work on the simplest level of demanding shorter hours, with men choosing to take part of their increasing productivity in the form of time off rather than of an increase in real income. It is part of the same demand that men, not themselves close to retirement and thus not faced with its financial and psychological hazards, press for ever earlier retirement "so that a man can do all those things in life you can't do while you're working." Among steelworkers we have found in conversation that employees from twenty-five to fifty-five almost unanimously advocate retirement commencing at fifty-five or earlier, blithely dismissing the inevitable economic questions with assertions that they will be able to "make out" and expectations that better stipends for the retired are just around the political corner.[4]

At a certain point, however, workers seem to want to buy leisure inside rather than outside the plant. No doubt, this in part reflects still operative conventions as to a proper working day, conventions

[4] Warren Peterson in a study of Kansas City schoolteachers found also this growing demand for early retirement, expressing boredom and defeatism about work as much as any specific desires for post-work leisure activities. (Unpublished doctoral disseration, Department of Sociology, University of Chicago, 1956). Many old-timers, however, both in schoolteaching and in the mills, continue to resist retirement, their grumpy habituation to work being the only structure their lives have. Cf. Eugene A. Friedmann and Robert J. Havighurst, *The Meaning of Work and Retirement* (Chicago: University of Chicago Press, 1954).

built into transportation, bookkeeping, and shift patterns. And in part men may fear to have too much time outside—time perhaps on which their wives could make demands. They may, like many of us in the business and professional strata, prefer to complain at home of their hard day's work while secretly profiting from its frivolities. At any rate, the unions in many advanced companies no longer spend all their energies resenting management abuses and encroachments, but can protect the processes of communication and interpersonal relationships in the plant (many grievers and shop stewards have become a kind of maintenance crew for sociability and gossip networks), and supervisory practices are forced to become more nearly commensurate with leisure-tinted images of what a proper workplace should be like. Many companies have taken the initiative on this front, moving for this as well as other reasons to pleasant suburbs, or to that Great American Suburb of the Southwest, thus luring employees out of the mills and offices designed in the pre-Raymond Loewy era.[5] Of course, there remain depressed industries and service trades which cannot afford the high overheads and mechanization of these new style-setters of "conspicuous production."

When Puritanism hit Merrie England, it had the effect, intensified by the subsequent industrial revolution, of pushing a larger and larger middle-class wedge between the Anglican gentry and the not yet Methodized workers, thus preserving only at the top and bottom of society certain pre-industrial pastimes and values. In this country, however, the middle-class wedge expanded until it embraced nearly the whole population, and the unaffected residues of older strata (as in the South) are small and uninfluential. Yet it is implicit in what we have said that the leisure which was once a fringe benefit now threatens to push work itself closer to the fringes

[5] Cf. E. L. Ullman, "Amenities as a Factor in Regional Growth," *Geographic Review*, XLIV (1954), p. 119. Among less mobile or redecoratable industries there is some resurgence today of management-sponsored recreation programs, which received a big boost during the "progressive management" movement of the 1920's. Indeed, what was worth a couple of chapters three decades ago (e.g., Lee K. Frankel and Alexander Fleisher, *The Human Factor in Industry* [New York: Macmillan, 1920], Chaps. 9 and 10) has now become a specialty for submanagers (e.g., Jackson M. Anderson, *Industrial Recreation* [New York: McGraw-Hill, 1955])—and one in which unions are beginning to stake out their own claims.

of consciousness and significance. In many facets of our national life, the anti-Puritan revolution seems to be almost accomplished (to be sure, among American workers Puritanism's hold, for ethnic and other reasons, was never complete).

Thus, the new situation confronts us with questions to which our own past is almost irrelevant, and the experience of less bountiful countries not much help either. We must ask, for instance, whether it is conceivable that, in a culture built on the industrial system, we can and should regard our still obligated work energies as mere payment for our consumer hedonism. Would we be happy if we attained a good racket, in which we never had to extend ourselves or never had to come into contact with any productive activity of men (other than voyeuristic contact through conducted tours of automatic factories)? It should be possible to give some empirical substance to speculation here through studies of standby musicians, pipefitters, railroad firemen, and others who get paid for not working, especially after they can no longer coast on motives of revenge against management, and "the system." As we were once unprepared for the factory, are we now not at least as unprepared for "the life of Riley," when it becomes no longer a dream but a barrier we have broken through?

Management and the workers both go on pretending that we needn't answer such questions. Management says that workers have lost the will to do an honest day's work, have lost ambition and the taste for workmanship. Workers argue that management wants to squeeze and speed them for the end of greater profits—not seeing the ideological unease their apparent indolence creates in a supervisory force itself no longer unequivocally committed to work-mindedness. None of this makes very much sense: it is using the rhetoric of the past to obscure the present, let alone the future. In *The Concept of the Corporation,* Peter Drucker comes to terms with some of this, showing how rearrangement of assembly lines into more individualized work groups can alleviate monotony and provide variety and idiosyncratic pacing of work. Fromm in *The Sane Society,* and Percival and Paul Goodman in *Communitas,* believe that radical reconstructions of the work process are necessary before it can be humanized and enlivened. The latter touch on the difficult problem of periodicity—of how to alternate challenge and routine

—a problem that will increase in importance as workflows become stabilized with automation, full employment, and a permanent war economy. In part, of course, these are matters beyond our limited assignment in this volume, but we cannot look at leisure without inquiring about its relation to work: is it escape, counterpoise, or possibly the managing partner, with work now the sleeping one?

WORK AND LEISURE IN THE LIFE-CYCLE

We know all too well some of the less amiable ways in which training for both work and leisure takes place in school—that pre-industrial waiting room to which our high productivity, our youth-centeredness, and many other forces consign the young. It is here, *inter alia,* that the future factory worker learns to define tasks set by authority as a test of his individual skill at evasion and of group cooperativeness in setting easily accessible norms and in punishing rate-busters. It is here that aspirations are whetted for consumption goods—and often blunted for other potential or historical goals. Creativity may sometimes find an outlet in hotrodding—a craft that may also serve the young factory worker as a subliminal protest against the monopolization of skilled jobs in the plant by the older men and against the middle-class mores and functional inefficiencies built into the vehicle by Detroit. Even while one is still in high school, part-time jobs may provide the wherewithal for a car, and also set the later life pattern of part-time service jobs held in addition to the steady but meaningless factory job in order to bring additional income in for the sake of a higher standard of living. The car, of course, also serves an as aid to sexual adventuring and general free-spending, which the young and unattached factory worker can today readily afford, what with the compression of ranks and the decline of older patterns of apprenticeship. What liquor was for an older, rougher, and more impoverished generation, gasoline (plus some liquor, too, of course) is for the contemporary young worker. He can also afford, though paying a token room and board to his mother, expensive (though not highfalutin) dates, trips, and tailormade suits.

But marriage comes early in the life-cycle of the industrial worker, and the costs which the scarcely risen paycheck must meet jump steadily with the acquisition of a family and a household.[6] Hotrodding is then likely to cease, and the worker will settle into a family car which he carefully maintains in its original form for the sake of its trade-in value—though he may take it for repairs to a friend who has retained the practiced ability to tinker with automobiles as an adult leisure specialty. Or he may drive to work in a clunker to which he devotes as little attention as possible so long as it runs. At this point, his house rather than his car is likely to claim his attention. Even half a century ago, according to Frederick Winslow Taylor's account of "Schmidt," the unreflective Dutchman whom he taught a better way of loading pig iron, this worker "upon wages of $1.15 a day . . . had succeeded in buying a small plot of ground . . . and was engaged in putting up the walls of a little house for himself in the morning before starting to work and at night after leaving."[7] It seems likely that Schmidt's model was not an urban bourgeois but rather a well-to-do peasant, the farm-boy newly come to the city, or the small-town artisan. This model is still alive among many factory workers today. They buy homes because they have never resigned themselves to the role of tenant and because they want a house and land as a bit of old-age security (including the security of activity).

Especially since World War II, many young married workers have kept mortgages low by living in tarpaper shacks or trailers or basements while accumulating above or around them what in four or five years will be at least a "decent," if not inspiring, shelter —not jerry-built but with little regard for the symbolic values real estate agents find or invent in dwellings. One of us has been engaged in this process in a working-class suburb of Gary, Indiana, to which subsequent settlers have come to build more imposing homes with bigger mortgages and some symbols of status, such as stone facing (which in such a Veblenian neighborhood must be justified by ref-

[6] Marvin Sussman has gathered data on how, in middle-class families, the parents help the young married couple to get started by tactful gifts of furniture and funds; in the working class, capital resources of this sort scarcely exist. "The Help Pattern in the Middle Class Family," *American Sociological Review*, XVIII (February 1953), pp. 22-28. For fuller treatment of consumption patterns in relation to the life-cycle, see David Riesman and Howard Roseborough, "Careers and Consumer Behavior," in Lincoln Clark, ed., *Consumer Behavior* (New York: New York University Press, 1955), pp. 1-18.

[7] *Scientific Management* (New York: Harper, 1911), pp. 43-44.

erence to insulating qualities and ease of maintenance and, in moments of honesty, the pacification of a style-conscious and insistent wife). But these later arrivals are not trying to catch up with any middle-class Joneses, having deliberately moved to an area where middle-class people are conspicuous by their absence and where they can get more land and a lower tax rate. For the men, at least, the primary fulfillment provided by the house is not dissimilar to that of the car: it is the tangible possession, with the feel of ownership or of "thing-manship."

While possessions and children are being accumulated, the steps in the ladder of plant seniority are likely to seem particularly slow and frustrating, and the ex-teen-ager who casually hired in may begin (like the auto workers Ely Chinoy describes in *Automobile Workers and the American Dream*) to wonder about some entrepreneurial activity which might allow escape from the plant altogether if it pays off (and minimally allow mitigating the pressure of his installment payments). He may spend his weekends repairing TV rather than looking at it, or (like some of the workers described in Charles Walker's *Steeltown*) driving a cab or truck for hauling, or servicing cars at a gas station rather than driving aimlessly about. This period may be the low point of his preoccupation with leisure within as well as outside the plant, for he may make a play for advancement or upgrading.

Only a good deal later will he have risen high enough in the pay-skill hierarchy, paid off enough of his investment in the hard goods of domesticity, and given his children, in the language of the labor movement, "a childhood for every child," so that he can resume the extensive and intensive preoccupation with leisure of his own adolescence and youth. At this point there may be a renewed interest in how much fun one can have at work. This is what in all probability one is going to be doing for the rest of one's days; one has what it takes, and one might as well enjoy it. For those numerous workers who love to eat and travel, rising standards of living and a plateau of obligations at this point usually mean more of the same traditional and conventional fare and faring: a classier motel, a more expensive steak (cooked as before). The children and grandchildren are enabled to enjoy expensive play equipment—bicycles, sports gear, camping.

Yet, for many, a fundamental dissatisfaction remains which one of us has called the "tradition of failure": the conviction of many older workers, including those who have nice homes, expensive cars, and children in college, that success in life is achieved only by men who manage to get out of the mill by the routes of small business, politics, or "some other good racket." America has taught them that the best things in life are not free. They are close enough to production and profits to know that the things are there for the asking—and to their unions to know how to ask. But they are also too Americanized to look favorably on mill work, no matter whether their standard of living is the envy of the lower ranks of the white-collar world.

LEISURE CLASS AND MASS

By the same token, it becomes increasingly difficult to distinguish their leisure from that of the rest of the country. Even worker suburbs *are* suburbs—very different (as Clark Kerr has seen in another connection) from the monolithic mining towns, lumber camps, or urban worker districts which encapsulate a distinctive working-class style and labor ideology. It is a commonplace that the mass consumption goods and the mass media tend to blur class lines, and tend, moreover, not only to foster filtering down of leisure-class patterns from the taste leaders at the top but also to promote uniformities from below. Thus, the casual garb of the worker off the job tends to merge with the "sincere" and unaffected garb of the office worker—and their wives may both read *McCall's* at the same beauty parlor.

Yet there remain certain distinctions. One of these may be summarized by noting that the worker, as a parvenu, tends to have a more unequivocal relation to consumer goods than do people who have had a longer exposure to them. One of us supervised a study which illustrates the point. Working-class and middle-class parents were interviewed concerning their attitudes toward TV: for the former, this was an extrapolation of radio and the movies, and an indubitably good *thing* in a world of things, whereas for many middle-class parents TV presented a problem in self-definition, as well as in its possibly harmful effects on children.[8] The working

[8] Cf. Margarete Midas, "Without TV," *American Quarterly*, III (1951), pp. 152-166.

class, for all that some of its attitudes resemble those of the idle rich of a generation ago, is still a long distance away from the plight of those who, bored by possessions, begin to collect ideas, diseases, or (as in Louis Kronenberger's witty novel, *Grand Right and Left*) people.

This adherence to the tangible, then, characterizes working-class leisure activities in a wide gamut: the garden harvest which, like the fishing catch, can be counted and weighed; the travel mileages and car horsepowers which can be compared; and sex (whether marital or not), drinking, sports, and betting, which are all felt as essentially palpable. To be sure, we do not want to exaggerate, after the fashion of D. H. Lawrence and other romantics, the lack of abstraction, nuance, and shadings of taste among factory workers. We know that even where the objects are the same, the meanings we assume to be attached to them are of course attached only to their human possessors and that there is great variety here. For a Mississippi-born Negro to own a car may be a pleasure only those who have experienced Jim Crow transportation can realize, and his gaudy Buick, bought on time in St. Louis or Detroit, may be not only a triumph over caste restrictions but also over a life without possessions—even repossessions. In contrast, the same car in the hands of a semiskilled high school graduate of high intelligence, a man who is filled with frustration and unspent energy as he leaves the plant and drives like mad through homebound traffic, may signify a still further resignation to a fate beyond his control within and outside the factory.

Beyond that, it is our impression that the simplicities of working-class leisure are under pressure not only from the tastes of the better educated strata as class consciousness and cultural encapsulation decline, but also from what we might term the "feminizing" of leisure. To be sure, this has not yet won much recognition in the all-male world of the factory, where the talk among the millhands, like their horseplay, defends a cherished masculine preserve, resembling the talk of a military post, a lodge, a pool room, or an all-male convention. Likewise, whenever the worker finds himself among other men in the working-class suburb or established working-class section of the metropolis, he can either talk shop or continue the other rather uninvolved talk—sports or sex or automobile talk—of the shop. So, too, a strike gives him the chance to choose, free of domestic prior commitment, between painting the garage or going fishing. However, as we know, the factory itself is increasingly invaded by women, no longer always segregated in separate departments. And we have also seen how the decor of the plant tends to become softer and less rugged, so that a foundry today often looks like a light industry of a generation ago.

More important still, in the outside world feminine influences are clearly increasing, as marriages, following the middle-class mode, become more companionate and less patriarchal; often the teen-age daughter first "brings up" her mother and then, in conspiracy with the latter, goes to work on Dad. Here again the situation of the factory worker today is reminiscent in certain respects of that of the nineteenth-century capitalist whose wife dragged him reluctantly toward "culture" and away from his "materialistic" preoccupations. The plant continues to be a refuge for those men who either cannot or do not want to acquire the sorts of "feminine" sensitivity and aspirations which go with more abstract forms of work and recreation. But such men, much as they may set the tone in mining or logging camp or open hearth, are seldom in the majority in a plant, and it follows that in-plant sociability does not always exclude (as it does, by tacit convention, on a hunting trip)[9] those leisure roles that involve women, including discussions of housebuilding and maintenance, movies and TV shows, home cooking (with trading of ethnic recipes), flower raising, and so on. Here, too, of course, the emphasis is on the tangible, but the ambit of domestic relationships involving the objects is wider.

Other changes, present and impending, within the factory point in the same direction. No longer does factory work concentrate attention on objects directly, on the hardness of the materials. Increasingly, apart from the maintenance and transportation crews, the production employees are engaged in communicating with each other concerning what the equipment is doing, and maintaining the proper relationships between intricately coordinated machines. Work itself becomes more abstract, more complex, more intellectual —hence, in the specialized sense of this paper, less "male." The

[9] Cf. Gregory F. Stone, "American Sports: Play and Dis-Play," *Chicago Review,* IX (1955), pp. 83-100.

physical feel for the work which allowed an old-time furnace tender to tell from a glance at a peephole if the heat was of proper quality gives way to the practiced utilization of instruments such as the spectroscope, and eventually to an electronic control system which provides on charts and dials a numerical and graphic overview of the whole production process. (All this is quite apart from the actual decline of manufacturing labor as a proportion of a workforce increasingly engaged in the tertiary trades, including the servicing of each other's leisure.)

Such developments imply that the class line in the plant, presently attenuated, is likely to become even less clear cut. Even now, the jobs of many production-line workers would allow them to wear shirts and ties, perhaps protected by lab-like smocks, and their pay would allow them access to the nicer cafeterias, rather than eating at a canteen or sitting on a machine or stool to open their lunchboxes and their thermoses. The dirt and noise and smell now associated with the production floor are as likely to disappear from the factory of the future as the shabby locker room and nondescript plant uniform of the blue-collar man. For a while, loyalties and traditions will make for friction if the worker tries to dress up in the plant and "act middle class." But we have already spoken of the decline of violence and of the general softening of manners (save in international relations and on TV!): as production-floor work becomes increasingly safe and comfortable, brawling within or outside the plant falls progressively into disrepute. Unlike the situation in Europe or South America, there is virtually no aristocracy to provide models for the working class which contrast sharply with general middle-class norms; indeed, such once-aristocratic sports as breeding pedigreed dogs, sailing, and horseback riding have come to be widespread among industrial workers as well as white-collar employees. And we should again remind the reader that this is a two-way traffic, so that lower-class manners are softening while the upper social strata complain of a loss of refinement, and their children wear bluejeans.

A PAUL BUNYAN OF THE SUPERMARKETS?

In a justly famous essay, Leo Lowenthal traced a decline in biographies of "heroes of production" in the *Saturday Evening Post* and a rise in biographies of "heroes of consumption" such as movie and sports celebrities; and even when magnates and statesmen are now discussed, he observed that it is their personalities and their non-work activities that are commented on:[10] leisure gives status to work, rather than the other way around. Likewise, it is our impression that there has been a change in heroes within the working-class community. A generation ago these were production heroes who brought their prestige with them out of the mill—supercraftsmen like the old hammer forge operators who could control the massive power of their tools to crack the crystal on a watch without damaging the works, and physical giants who could lift more than anyone else in the plant and win more fights in front of the tavern. As part of the same setting, the big steel mills and metal-working plants were the most impressive aspect of the workers' communities, dwarfing even the cathedrals built by the massed savings of the various ethnic enclaves.

Today, in contrast, though the mills and the oil-cracking plants are still impressive, industry no longer favors River-Rouge-type displays of concentrated power but rather dispersed one-story plants no more imposing than one of the new suburban shopping centers. For competing symbols of glamor, workers have access to their own consumer hard goods, to the big screens of Hollywood and the small ones of TV. By the same token, the worker today can bring status into the plant from the bright and various world outside—from his extravagant hunting or extensive traveling, as well as from his activities in the union or in local politics. Within the plant, the general upgrading of industrial workers, the bureaucratization of wage rates and promotions (and union control or influence over these), and the development of finer gradations so that the top men are not so clearly distinguishable from the rest, de-emphasize the place of status won within as against status won outside. Elton Mayo, writing a generation ago of the factory as a restorative and stabilizer for clique members against the disruptions of the surrounding anomic neighborhoods, could hardly have anticipated the degree to which the factory, despite the continuing growth of its

[10] See Lowenthal, "Biographies in Popular Magazines," *Radio Research, 1942-1943*, Paul F. Lazarsfeld and Frank Stanton, eds. (New York: Duell, Sloan and Pearce, 1944), p. 507.

ancillary services to workers and their communities, would lose its position of emotional dominance as the workers' Americanization and often pat sophistication in leisure-time affairs proceeded.

This shift is part of a larger one in the forms by which the drive for social mobility are expressed. At one time, one gained status only from one's place on the land, and in the kin nexus which related one to the land. The factory accompanied a change to more portable forms of status, yet it was itself at first tied to a particular place by need for water power or coal or transport, and the work-group was anchored within the plant to stationary machinery. Commensurately, one rose in status by climbing the occupational ladder within the plant, meanwhile consolidating one's position in the town through family alliances, an impressive house, and visible civic and parochial activities. Today, as we have seen, the factory is free of close "ecological" ties to real estate and can move in search of amenities defined as such in a national inherently portable system of "consumer" values. Under these conditions, the younger workers, high-school trained, become quickly impatient with their slow progress within the plant hierarchy—but this hierarchy is no longer the only one they see in front of them. In nonwork activities, they already have more experience and expertise than many "senior" men; and in these, "around end" as it were, they look for roads to a more personal as well as more portable kind of status. A millhand today may feel he has it made if, for example, he can afford winter as well as summer vacations. His leisure specialties may bring him income or prestige or both. If he takes a hand in local politics, it may be less out of class-conscious ideology or out of a desire to leave the mill for an easier life, and more because he now has time for the great game of politics, as well as the knowhow to profit from its incidental perquisites. If he moves from the old working-class part of the city to a suburb on its perimeter, he is again freeing himself from the need to have access to many factory gates, counting on his car and his union to provide him with a job within a reasonable orbit; in his new suburb (as among the Park Forest "transients" described by William H. Whyte, Jr., in *Fortune*), he will be judged as it were "horizontally" by his style of life rather than "vertically" by his occupation.

In this new perspective, leisure, which was once a residual compensation for the tribulations of work, may become what workers recover from at work (as children recover from vacations at school)! A worker relates his work to his life as follows, according to Fred H. Blum: "The routine keeps your mind well grounded . . . and makes you a stable citizen."[11] Work may appear as a last remnant of rootedness, of "grounding," in a world of such mobility that goals, including the nature of status itself, are being continuously redefined in experiences away from work.

Were he alive today, Veblen would almost surely feel disheartened at this prospect; it would seem to him as if the rationalities of production had been defeated by the irrationalities of consumption and leisure so that even skilled workers, his favorite cadre, had joined the apostles of wastemanship rather than workmanship. Yet he might also conclude that the older form of the drive for status—the source of meaning for many but of suffering for most—had lost something of its imperative quality. No doubt, this replacement is partly fatalistic, reflecting growing rigidities in the social and political structure of a garrison state, but does it not also reflect a greater maturity, a greater mobility of the imagination? (No doubt also, before we look too far ahead, we must remember the enormous distance still to go toward equalization: to move, for instance, from the noisy tenements of Chicago's Black Belt, with its population swollen by postwar waves of immigration from the Delta and other rural and small-town areas of the Illinois Central's South, to the neat well-off, well-kept homes of craft-conscious German and Swedish workers in Milwaukee is to change worlds. Yet these worlds even now communicate with one another, and all American experience, all industrial experience, shows the fabulous speeds with which social distances can be annihilated or reduced to marginal and even nostalgic tokens.)

Let us assume, beyond continuing equalizations along the lines here intimated—between the social classes, between men and women, young and old, rural and urban—the continued full employment and prosperity on which they considerably rest, and that this will continue to put unionized factory workers above even our changing definitions of poverty. Let us assume, too, that we continue to opt for increased productivity as well as increased time off.

[11] *Toward a Democratic Work Process* (New York: Harper, 1953), p. 97.

Does this presently visible potentiality of "nonwork" for variety and mobility—in homebuilding, domestic handicrafts, travel, organizational activity, sports, spectatorship, and even part-time entrepreneurship—provide an infinitely expandable package deal for the satisfying expenditure of time and energy and for the attainment of an adequate identity? Or are we coming to an era when workers have all the housing they care for, and can no longer pour energies into homebuilding? When possessions no longer lure them, when travel palls? No doubt, adult educators water at the mouth at the prospect—for they are in the business of selling intangibles for which the market is totally elastic. Yet how many workers are going to read this volume, concerned as it is with "their" problems and prospects?

The future seems "impossible," whichever way we look at it. Leisure marches on, while understanding of its import escapes these reporters, and planful invention and design of its opportunities escape all of us.

· VI ·

THE ECONOMIC ENVIRONMENT IN HUMAN RELATIONS RESEARCH

BY ABRAHAM J. SIEGEL
Massachusetts Institute of Technology

Human relations research is the recent product of one approach to analysis of man and work in modern industrial society. Some statements of this approach suggest vast scope and diverse perspectives for exploration.[1] The actual framework is much less comprehensive. Its features can be succinctly specified.

The focus of human relations research in industry is generally confined to the "social system" of the factory—or even more narrowly, the small group—and the relations existing among its parts.[2] Research questions are sparked by departures from a norm of harmonious relations among managed and managers within such systems, and studies seek to explain (and inferentially to eliminate) sources of these "problem" attitudes and actions in industry.[3] Expla-

[1] See, for example, Robert Tannenbaum, "An Evaluative Focus on Human Relations" (Working Paper for the Tenth Annual Industrial Relations Research Conference sponsored by the Labor Market Research Committee, Social Science Research Council, and the Industrial Relations Center, University of Minnesota May, 17-18, 1954), p. 6.

[2] William F. Whyte *et al.*, *Money and Motivation* (New York: Harper, 1955) p. 218.

[3] The description of the human relations field which Arensberg in a recent survey essay suggests as "best" is the "scientific study of the sources of unrest in labor and management relations, that is, the study of the problems of industrial relations." See Conrad M. Arensberg, "Behavior and Organization: Industrial Studies," in *Social Psychology at the Crossroads*, John H. Rohrer and Muzafer Sherif, eds. (New York: Harper, 1951), p. 330.

nations to account for industrial unrest are sought *within* the organizations in which men work.[4] Finally, human relations policy proposals aiming at the amelioration of conflict are similarly directed almost exclusively within the establishment and emphasize the strategic significance of leadership styles, communication patterns, work flows, participation, etc., in effecting cooperative industrial relations.[5]

Most criticisms of human relations research can be classified and their potential impact evaluated in relation to this basic approach. Some criticisms are easily countered without changing the framework. The charge, for example, that the human relationist has, in concentrating on the management unit, neglected to study human relations in the trade union can be—and to some extent already has been[6]—met with no great strain to the fundamental framework. Or take questions about unstated biases, and idealized good societies and charges that advocacy and analysis are intertwined. These are important and salutary caveats (for any research framework), but once again, while revisions in the human relationist's normative assertions about harmonious equilibrium might extend the role of constructive conflict in his analysis or modify his set of policy prescriptions, they do not per se vitiate the utility of his basic research framework. A third set of criticisms presents greater difficulty, for it suggests an essential modification in the human relations approach. This criticism questions the adequacy of generalizations about internal social systems which are wrought without regard to external environmental variables affecting these systems. This chapter centers on "environmentalist" criticism.[7]

[4] For illustrative description of this internalized vantage point adopted for human relations theorizing see George C. Homans, "A Conceptual Scheme for the Study of Social Organization," *American Sociological Review*, XII (February 1947), p. 13; William F. Whyte, "Framework for the Analysis of Industrial Relations: Two Views," *Industrial and Labor Relations Review*, III (April 1950); and Conrad M. Arensberg, *op. cit.*, p. 337.

[5] See Chris Argyris, *The Present State of Research in Human Relations in Industry* (New Haven: Labor and Management Center, Yale University, 1954) for an extensive inventory of contemporary theoretical activity and derivative policy propositions in American human relations research in industry.

[6] See, for example, William F. Whyte, *Pattern for Industrial Peace* (New York: Harper, 1951) and Leonard R. Sayles and George Strauss, *The Local Union: Its Place in the Industrial Plant* (New York: Harper, 1953).

[7] External environment refers here to the extra-plant aggregation of economic

THE "ENVIRONMENTALIST" CRITIQUE

Summary of the Criticism[8]

Environmentalist criticism reflects essentially a basic uneasiness about the capacity of the human relations framework to provide full and adequate answers to questions asked about the underlying uniformities and differences in motivational, attitudinal, and behavioral patterns and relations of men at work in modern industrial society.[9] Limiting the formal context for generalization about the sources of worker unrest to the "manageable analytical unit" of the plant runs the serious risk of assigning an unwarranted explanatory autonomy to proximate, internal variables and structural relationships. The environmentalist critic suggests that the human relationist's strategic variables are themselves derivative in nature.

---

and sociopolitical factors within which behavioral patterns and relationships of managed and managers at work are structured and developed. It is contrasted with the less inclusive set of variables internal to the plant emphasized in human relations research.

[8] The general line of argument summarized here may be found, put with varying degrees of intensity, in Herbert Blumer, "Sociological Theory in Industrial Relations," *American Sociological Review,* XII (June 1947), pp. 271-278; Wilbert E. Moore, "Current Issues in Industrial Sociology," *American Sociological Review,* XII (December 1947), pp. 651-657; "Industrial Sociology: Status and Prospects," *American Sociological Review,* XIII (August 1948), pp. 382-391; Harold Sheppard, "Managerial Sociology," (Doctoral dissertation, University of Wisconsin, 1948); *Psychology of Labor-Management Relations,* Arthur W. Kornhauser, ed., (Champaign: Industrial Relations Research Association, 1949), pp. 3-4, 66, 83-84 and 103-106; John T. Dunlop, "Framework for the Analysis of Industrial Relations: Two Views," *Industrial and Labor Relations Review,* III (April 1950), pp. 383-393 and in Comments by Bakke, Brown, Fisher, and Kerr, pp. 402-412; F. H. Harbison and J. R. Coleman, *Goals and Strategy in Collective Bargaining* (New York: Harper, 1951), pp. 118 *ff.*; Robert C. Stone, "Conflicting Approaches to the Study of Worker-Manager Relations," *Social Forces,* XXXI (December 1952), pp. 117-124; Jessie Bernard, "Current Research in the Sociology of Conflict," (Working paper prepared for the International Sociological Association meetings in Liege, August 24-September 1, 1953); Robert Tannenbaum, *op. cit.,* pp. 21-23; and Isidor Chein, "The Environment as a Determinant of Behavior," *The Journal of Social Psychology,* XXXIX (February 1954), pp. 115-127.

[9] There are, in addition, those manifestations of discomfort, often implicitly intertwined with and logically related to this basic uneasiness, which suggest that many questions which press for answers are denied even the asking in a framework which cuts off its formal analytical probing at the edges of the workgroup or the gates of the plant.

Occurrence probabilities, limits to their variability, or limits to the impact of their variation upon peace or conflict results will depend upon external environmental supports or constraints which impinge upon the analytical microcosm. The human relationist thus excludes precisely those variables which give systematic character to the phenomena he microscopically inspects. In so doing he fetters himself too frequently to descriptive generalization after the fact—to "how's" more often than to "why's." And in neglecting the strategic clues which reference to extraplant variables provides concerning the nature as well as the extent of industrial unrest, he is gainsaid the opportunity to fashion adequate predictive (or in policy application, prescriptive) explanation.

Environmental Variables That Appear To Affect Patterns of Peace or Protest

Industrial relations are not structured in a vacuum. Worker-employer relationships are initiated and develop in a matrix of physical, economic, political, and cultural surroundings. They are circumscribed by an interrelated set of legacies of the past, elements of the present, and anticipations of the future. The following paragraphs catalogue some of the contours of the industrial environment which shape human relations in the workplace:

The specific environment—size of the plant and company; seasonal and cyclical stability of its production pattern; volume, nature, and rate of technical change (and related ratio of capital investment per worker); quality and composition of its jobs; comparative cost position; nature of the product market (expansion or contraction, sensitivity to the business cycle, responsiveness of market demand to price changes); nature of the labor market (quality and supply of the work force available, percentage of the labor force in the area employed by the company, local wage levels); nature of the union dealt with (institutional security of the union, presence or absence of rival unionism or internal factionalism, degree of bargaining autonomy the union can exercise, ideological commitments of its leadership, degree of political involvement); role of the company as pattern-setter or pattern-follower; age and origins of the bargaining relationship.

The broader environment—community's pro- or anti-union complexion; procedural and substantive content of past and prevailing labor legislation; level of general economic activity; the broad stage of the economy's relative incipiency or maturity of industrial development; the pressures, motivations, and groups or agencies assuming organizational responsibility for industrialization; the historical timing of industrialization; the ideological organizing principles of the culture (egalitarian liberalism, autocratic paternalism, etc.).

For any two situations we may care to compare or generalize about at a given point in industrial time and in a given society, there may be marked differences in any one or a combination of some of the specific extra-plant environmental variables. For any two situations compared *over* time in a given society (e.g., worker protest in early nineteenth- as against mid-twentieth-century England) or for any two situations compared at a given point of chronological time in *different* societies (e.g., industrial relations behavior and the nature of worker protest in the United States as against Russia or India of 1956), there may be marked differences in the *total* environmental context. These differences never enter explicitly into the formulation of human relations theory, but they may be indispensable in helping to account for the kinds of "problems" (or for the tactics and forms of expression of the problems) which will confront differently situated relationships. By providing diverse directors, restraints, or supports, they will prescribe sometimes more, sometimes less, coercive limits for the building of industrial peace or the perpetuation of industrial conflict. By ascribing varying roles to worker, employer, and state in the rule-making and enforcing relationships, they will shape the whole structure of the web of rules relating workers to one another, to the employer, to the state, and to the productive process. The following two sections outline some illustrative hypotheses relating environmental factors to the nature and extent of worker unrest.[10]

ENVIRONMENT AND THE NATURE OF INDUSTRIAL UNREST

The external environment may shape decisively the *kinds of* problems about which worker grievances will center:

In an auto plant . . . the large number of employees within a single establishment, the extreme specialization of job content, the large number of employees usually required on each job classification and within easily interchangeable groups of jobs, and the constant process of technologic

[10] See also suggestive references in Harold L. Wilensky's Chapter III, this volume.

change and managerial improvement all mean that the handling of individual wage-rate and classification problems and the application of seniority rules are likely to be important sources of grievances. On the other hand, in the hotel and restaurant industries, in building service, and in the building trades, the dispersion of the work force among many employers, so that there may be only one or a few workers on each classification in an establishment, and the irregularity of employment or the rapid turnover among both employers and employees mean that length of service has little meaning in governing job tenure.[11]

In periods of sharply declining levels of economic activity we may expect that the progressing downswing will more likely be accompanied by a rash of unrest over employer-proposed wage reductions than by union protests for wage increases. And the sources of industrial unrest may be quite different in the incipient stages of industrial development than in the mature industrial society. The latter has problems of its own, but it has in large part digested or eliminated the labor problems which arise from the drastic disruption of tradition—the shift from one way of life to another—inherent in the recruitment and commitment of a nonagricultural work force in the transition to industrialism.

Environmental factors may help account for *tactics and manifestations* of protest as well as for problem-likelihoods. The appeal of the "quickie" strike in longshoring, for example, can be explained in large part by its tactical effectiveness given the nature of the industry.[12] Kuhn accounts for the greater participation of Australian workers in short-duration stoppages by reference to the role of the Australian arbitration system and the degree of trade union political involvement.[13] And the substitutions of machine-breaking for collec-

[11] Van D. Kennedy, "Grievance Negotiation," in *Industrial Conflict*, Arthur Kornhauser, Robert Dubin, Arthur M. Ross, eds. (New York: McGraw-Hill, 1954), p. 284. See also John T. Dunlop and James J. Healy, *Collective Bargaining* (Homewood, Ill.: Richard D. Irwin, 1953), pp. 74 *ff.*, for extensive generalization relating external environmental variables and problems in collective bargaining.

[12] Profitability depends on a quick turnaround and a minimum of down time in port. This knowledge and the knowledge that the loading or discharging of cargo remained to be completed, whatever the outcome of the job action—and often at overtime rates—made this already psychologically appealing weapon virtually cost-free to the union.

[13] The arbitration system has weakened collective bargaining but has helped shorten disputes; further, the high degree of trade union political involvement and the concomitant neglect of local problems frequently compels the dramatization of worker discontent via the short work stoppage which becomes in

tive bargaining in the textile industry in early nineteenth-century England[14] or of mass petitions in Czarist Russia and labor turnover ("striking with the feet") in Soviet Russia for the strike[15] are more readily explained by reference to external environmental constraints than by the internal organization of industry.

Finally, organizational forms which claim proprietorship and control of worker protest change over time and are cast in alternative molds. If we seek explanation for these alternative channels through which worker discontent is expressed, manipulated, controlled, and structured, it is again to the broader patterns of industrialization and the cultural and political backdrops against which these develop that we must go in our search for explanatory variables. In Britain, for example, changes in industry structure, in levels of literacy, in political rules of the game, and in the general level of material welfare can be related readily, on the labor organization side, to the shift from an uncoordinated multitude of poorly-financed, short-lived, and ephemeral competing organizations, "localized, atomized, fractionalized," to the centralized, formalized, legitimized, and viable labor movement of today—cohesive, well-financed, concerned with the survival and continuity of organization, bargaining at industry-wide levels, etc. But the model of British labor organization, in turn, may be irrelevant in the context of other societies differently situated:

> British industrialization came early, was initiated "from below" by a middle class sparked by the Protestant Ethic, and proceeded at a moderate rate. British capitalism was the model for the classical portrait of the self-regulating market mechanism, organized in keeping with the strong individualist, laissez-faire principles of economic liberalism. British labor organization in turn developed after a certain fashion.

Contrast this, for example, with Japanese industrialization which came

---

this instance as much a manifestation of protest against the union as against the employer. See James W. Kuhn, "Grievance Machinery and Strikes in Australia," *Industrial and Labor Relations Review*, VIII (January 1955), pp. 169-176.

[14] See E. J. Hobsbawm, "The Machine Breakers," *Past and Present*, I (February 1952) and Frank O. Darvall, *Popular Disturbances and Public Order in Regency England* (Oxford: Oxford University Press, 1934).

[15] See S. P. Turin, *From Peter the Great to Lenin* (London: P. S. King and Son, 1935); Isaac Deutcher, "Russia," in *Comparative Labor Movements*, Walter Galenson, ed. (New York: Prentice-Hall, 1952), pp. 480 *ff*.

late, was initiated "from above" by a feudal oligarchy sparked by a nationalist ethic, and which proceeded at a more rapid rate. Japanese capitalism entailed state organization, direction, and controls from the very first. It bore no stamp of a liberal legacy or of a self-dependent-worker ideology. Japanese labor organization there was, but not out of the British mold. The structuring of the industrial labor force came not in the form of a "labor movement" but rather in the form of an employer-controlled and state-enforced feudal paternalism.[16]

ENVIRONMENT AND THE EXTENT OF INDUSTRIAL UNREST

One conjuncture of environmental circumstances may support a minimization of industrial unrest; another may conduce and almost coerce the parties toward a relatively high proneness to conflict.

Kerr summarizes typical environmental circumstances surrounding peaceful collective bargaining systems analyzed in the National Planning Association's *Causes of Industrial Peace* series:

> A medium-sized company with a steady production pattern and subject to moderate technological advance; interesting and responsible jobs; an efficient company with an expanding market and administered prices; a company which is firmly established in a multi-industry community which has a tractable labor force and wage levels which can readily be met in accordance with industry standards; a community which is accustomed to collective bargaining; a secure union with stable leaders and a homogeneous membership; a wage pattern which the parties can use as a guide; some local autonomy for both parties; a system which is well-established, and leaders on both sides who are experienced.[17]

This is indeed a favorable set of environmental circumstances within which to fashion a peaceful, constructive union-management relationship. We could posit that given such a set of environmental factors, the likelihood of industrial peace will generally exceed that of industrial conflict. This provides an important first clue; it does not suggest that a permissive environment will per se and invariably cause peace. It is precisely at this juncture of analysis that we must look further to the attitudinal and internal organizational variables

[16] Clark Kerr and Abraham Siegel, "The Structuring of the Labor Force in Industrial Society: New Dimensions and New Questions," *Industrial and Labor Relations Review*, VIII (January 1955), p. 160.

[17] National Planning Association, *Fundamentals of Labor Peace: A Final Report* (Washington: The Association, 1953), p. 60.

to which the human relationist directs his entire formal attention. At this second order of generalization, these may assume vital tactical significance in achieving and partially explaining cooperative relations. The effectiveness of appropriate tactical maneuvers ought not, however, to displace from view the strategic significance of environmental supports. Kerr and Fisher stress this analytical oversight in their criticism of what they have termed "plant" sociology:

In the Pattern for Industrial Peace, . . . Whyte detailed over a decade of industrial relations history with almost no reference to external factors. This was possible, in part, because of the very nature of the environment within which the plant operated. The Inland Steel Company and the United Steelworkers of America removed one of the most outward looking issues from discussion at the plant level—the settlement of wages. There was full employment and profits were good. If, for example, the company had been a marginal one, or there had been a period of mass unemployment, or the union Communist-dominated, or the work casual, it would not have been possible so to ignore developments outside the plant society. . . . Which environments are more and which less conducive to good human relations and thus good industrial relations? This is a question to which the plant sociologist has not yet addressed himself; and it will be difficult for him to do so without altering his concentration on the plant as a largely self-contained society. If he did, it would probably develop that there are types of industrial relations and not just stages. In discovering types of industrial relations, it would be found that some are not open to improvement by an increase in social skills but only by an alteration of the external environment.[18]

Or we might ask why it is that some industries (like mining and maritime and longshoring) are chronically conflict-ridden in many parts of the world while others (like clothing, agriculture, and trade) are persistently peaceful. Again the strategic explanation for these persisting differences in interindustry proneness to conflict seems to lie in the industrial environment rather than in internal interaction patterns or differences in face-to-face relations or communications channels:

[18] Clark Kerr and Lloyd Fisher, "Plant Sociology: The Elite and the Aborigines," (to be published in *Common Frontiers of the Social Sciences,* Paul Lazarsfeld and Mirra Komarovsky, eds.). See also the "reply" essay by Conrad M. Arensberg and Geoffrey Tootel, "Plant Sociology: Real Contributions," to be published in the same volume.

It seems more likely that some situations are structured against good face-to-face relations and that this structure is the more basic cause and source of the more basic changes. The climate of face-to-face relations may be one way of testing and of describing the degree of conflict or cooperation in an industry, and there may be occasions when manipulation of these relations alone will bring great changes, but it seems unlikely that the peace in government agencies and the warfare on the waterfront are due primarily to the universal superiority in human-relations techniques of government bureaucrats over stevedoring contractors. Even if this were the case, it would still need to be explained why government draws to it a more skillful elite than the longshore industry. Labor relations may be a mirror in which the employer sees his own reflection . . . but why then are employers more decent in one industry than another? At this point some reference needs to be made to the industrial environment. *Causa causae est causa causati.*[19]

Or, finally, it makes good sense to relate the cyclical and secular patterns of aggregate strike activity in a country to the considered tactics of trade union leaders and to the strategic relationship these bear to the general level of business activity and to the institutional security provided the trade union.[20]

REBUTTAL OF THE CRITICISM

Environmentalist critics suggest, in sum, that the external environment will affect the sources, manifestations, and organization of worker protest. Together, these define the nature of unrest. Differences in the nature of protest will in turn be reflected in differences in the volume, extent, and impact of industrial unrest. Given this

[19] Clark Kerr and Abraham Siegel, "The Interindustry Propensity to Strike—An International Comparison," in *Industrial Conflict, op. cit.*, pp. 199-200. To explain these interindustry differences, the location of the worker in society and, as secondary influence, the nature of the job appeared to elucidate the behavior of most of the industries surveyed for most of the time periods covered better than any of the alternative theories which were examined. (Pp. 196-202.)

[20] See Albert Rees, "Industrial Conflict and Business Fluctuations," in *Industrial Conflict, op. cit.*, pp. 213-220; Arthur M. Ross and Donald Irwin, "Strike Experience in Five Countries, 1927-1947: An Interpretation," *Industrial and Labor Relations Review*, IV (April 1951), pp. 323-342; and K. Forchheimer, "Some International Aspects of the Strike Movement," *Bulletin of the Oxford University Institute of Statistics*, X (January and September 1948), pp. 9-24 and 294-304.

interdependence, it is hazardous to generalize about the causes and extent of industrial peace or conflict without explicit use of external environmental variables.

The criticism is parried by the human relationist in several ways:[21] (1) Limiting the unit of analysis is methodologically sound. To concentrate attention on a "big" picture prevents the testing of conclusions experimentally and makes intensive examination impossible. We must develop refined theory affording precise predictability within limited scope and then proceed to modify and reshape such small-scale generalization to make it serviceable in broader areas. (2) Science consists of the "careful and complete description of the mere facts." It concerns itself only with "how's" and never with "why's." (3) All-encompassing frameworks have in the past proved relatively fruitless. Attempts to take account of a host of economic or cultural environmental variables as these affect industrial relations have come up only with vague, general theory which is of little or no value in specific instances. (4) Environmental studies have been grossly negligent and inadequate in dealing appropriately with psychological factors which are best elucidated in the interrelationship of variables which small group analysis emphasizes. (5) Human relations research has not "neglected" external environmental factors. It takes these as "givens" and observes rather their influences only as these are translated into specific items of observed behavior within the social system of the work groups. (6) Finally, environmentalist critics have erred in their designation of the "strategic determinants" of worker behavior. External industrial environmental factors are inflexible and not easily altered—whatever the prevailing political or economic systems in which modern industry may be contained. Hence truly strategic determinants, the ones we might be able to change "in order to create a new industrial society," are internal. The "internal collaborative environment of the plant" is not alone the most amenable focus methodologically; it is the truly important one pragmatically.

[21] See, for example, William F. Whyte, "Framework. . . ," *op. cit.;* George C. Homans, *op. cit.*, and "Industrial Harmony as a Goal," in *Industrial Conflict, op. cit.*, p. 53; Conrad M. Arensberg, *op. cit.;* and Delbert C. Miller, "Discussion" of Wilbert E. Moore, "Industrial Sociology: Status and Prospects," *op. cit.*, pp. 394-395.

CONCLUSIONS: GENERALIZATION IN HUMAN RELATIONS RESEARCH

Much of what is suggested in the replies of the human relationist to criticisms of the environmentalist is valid. But the human relationist never dispels completely the reservations which linger about the strategic significance of the body of theory he has accumulated as suggested answers to his questions on causes of or correctives for industrial unrest. Nor does he dismiss the reservations which linger about the time horizons which his answers can encompass, or about the degree of transferability inhering in his answers, or about the number of relevant questions in industrial relations which are neither asked nor answered.

It is unquestionably true that it is easier to deal more intensively with the small, manageable unit of the plant than with the big picture which would incorporate the external milieu (and changes over time in that milieu) in which "men at work" are reared, live, and act in capacities other than worker or supervisor or employer or union leader. And it is equally true that generally it is easier to manipulate the internal environment of the plant than to effect change in the concatenation of sociopolitical, economic, or cultural institutions, forces, and pressures external to the plant. But what is most amenable to investigation or apprehension is not always the most reliable source of or the shortest cut to understanding and, unhappily, what is most susceptible to easy manipulation is not always the most relevant guide to effective control. Nor should we lament too readily the irrevocable fixity of the external environment, for as Myers has argued, some of its components can be changed over a period of time to improve the chances for industrial peace if this is desired.[22]

It is also true that science is concerned with "how's"—but only as a first, not an exclusive, step toward understanding. To ask for causation, for principles, and ultimately for policy is to go beyond the "how's" and enter the domain of the "why's." Human relations research has not avoided suggesting answers to "why" questions: Why is productivity high in Plant *A* and low in *B*? Why do we find cooperative worker-employer relations at *X* but not at *Y*? What

[22] See National Planning Association, *op. cit.*, pp. 92-99, for a discussion of the range of fixity in industrial environment as this relates to industrial peace.

it has done is to seek for generalization about cause-effect interrelationships in a rather narrow context.

And finally, it cannot be denied that, at best, theorizing in a broader framework has produced no better than what Gerschenkron has called "half-truth generalizations"—theories which do not afford precision of predictability in the specific instance. But can the human relationist claim even this measure of cross-cut half-truth transferability for his body of accumulated "if . . . then's"? The lack of precision in individual prediction which is illustrated by Goode and Fowler's[23] findings of the effective realization of management's formal goals in the small feeder plant in the automobile industry despite low worker morale could undoubtedly be replicated in other instances, for inasmuch as the human relationist formulates his theory "environment given," he can claim transferability for his findings only in similarly situated cases. This is legitimate and useful, but it comprises at best a limited portion of the answers we seek in industrial relations. How does one proceed beyond this to reshape and modify small group theory to make it serviceable to other small groups differently situated or for "broader areas" without extending the human relationist's "total situation"?

Arensberg[24] notes in commenting on the Goode and Fowler findings (and those of Harbison and Dubin in their study of collective bargaining at General Motors and Studebaker): "Both cases correlate psychological and behavioral by-products with the internal organizational differences. They differ from the other industrial sociologists, whom they criticize, *merely* in extending the chain of causation back a step into the larger environment." [Italics added.]

In that "merely" lies the nub of environmentalist criticism. To the extent that human relations research has rectified earlier disregard of the internal work group in industrial relations analysis, to the extent that it insists on seeing in details of a miniscule microcosm the details of the world, it bars the path to full explanation of industrial relations behavior and limits the range of generalization about man and work in modern industrial society. Whyte concludes a recent essay on the small group and the larger organization with this caveat:

[23] William J. Goode and Irving Fowler, "Incentive Factors in a Low Morale Plant," *American Sociological Review*, XIV (1949), pp. 618-624.

[24] Conrad M. Arensberg, *op. cit.*, p. 343.

There is no point to studying the over-all organizational structure unless we can trace out its impact upon particular individuals and groups. *Nor is there any point in studying the small group as if it operated in a vacuum.* . . . [Division of labor is necessary but] the researcher must not proceed in hermetically sealed compartments.

The social psychologist interested in small groups must be fully aware of the work going on in the larger structures. Otherwise he will ascribe to factors within the group influences that really impinge upon the group from outside. . . .

If research proceeds simultaneously in both areas, we will learn that certain characteristic forms of organizational structure are associated with certain specified types of behavior in small groups within that structure. Then, if we wish to modify behavior within the group, we will recognize that it will sometimes be necessary, in order to effect significant modifications, to make changes in the over-all structure of the organization *first.*[25]

The environmentalist critic of human relations research in industry "merely" suggests that it is myopic to neglect the logical extrapolation of Whyte's caveat: What the large organization is to the small group, the external environment is to the large organization.

[25] William F. Whyte, "Small Groups and Large Organizations," in *Social Psychology at the Crossroads, op. cit.,* pp. 311-312. Emphasis is Whyte's.

PART III

INDUSTRIAL ORGANIZATIONS: THEORY AND RESEARCH

· VII ·

AUTHORITY

BY HERBERT A. SIMON
Carnegie Institute of Technology

Without disputing the right of anyone else to use words as he pleases, I should like to state what I shall mean by *authority* in the remainder of this essay.

An individual accepts authority when he sets himself a general rule that permits the communicated decision of another to guide his own choice (i.e., to serve as a premise of that choice) independently of his judgment of the correctness or acceptability of the premise.[1]

It should be observed that it is a *definition,* not an empirical statement about behavior. Hence to label the definition "the acceptance theory of authority" and to describe it as "hedonistic," as has been done by some recent writers, is nonsense.[2] A definition is not a theory of anything, but a choice of word usage. Nor does the definition carry any particular implications for the motivation of the individual who accepts authority.

If we use the term "influence" to denote any change in behavior induced in one person by one or more others, then authority is one of the forms of influence, the other (persuasion) being change

[1] For a fuller discussion, see the author's *Administrative Behavior* (New York: Macmillan, 1947), p. 125; his *Public Administration* (New York: Knopf, 1950), pp. 180-182; and Chester I. Barnard's *The Functions of the Executive* (Cambridge: Harvard University Press, 1938), p. 163.

[2] See, for example, Harold Koontz and Cyril O'Donnell, *Principles of Management* (New York: McGraw-Hill, 1955), pp. 49-52.

induced by information and conviction. In any concrete instance, authority is unlikely to be observed in pure form, but, instead, is usually liberally admixed with persuasion.[8]

MOTIVATIONS FOR THE ACCEPTANCE OF AUTHORITY

Having settled definitional questions, we come to the real problems with which a study of authority in organizations must deal. First, under what circumstances and to what extent do individuals accept authority as a basis for their choices and behavior? Second, what motivates individuals to accept authority? Third, what are the consequences of an authority relation for those who exercise it and for those who accept it? Since our primary concern here is with the questions of policy and value that stem from the phenomena of authority, I shall proceed directly to the second and third questions.

What are the motivations for acceptance of authority? There are at least four that are of considerable importance:

1. *Rewards and Sanctions*

Authority is accepted because the person exercising it can attach pleasant or unpleasant consequences to action through the system of rewards and sanctions. (I will use the term "sanctions" to refer generically to both rewards and negative sanctions.) The most important sanctions of managers over workers in industrial organizations are (a) power to hire and fire, (b) power to promote and demote, and (c) incentive rewards.

The management of an industrial concern has these sanctions at its immediate disposal to a greater or lesser degree depending, among other things, upon alternative opportunities open to employees and upon strength of employee unions. In addition, society, through its legal system and courts, lends to members of industrial organizations other sanctions whose exercise is based on the law of contracts and property and upon special rights defined by statute (e.g., wage and hour legislation).

In the employer-employee relation the employer by no means

[8] On the broader concept, influence, see Herbert A. Simon, "Notes on the Observation and Measurement of Political Power," *Journal of Politics*, XV, (November 1953), pp. 500-516; James G. March, "An Introduction to the Theory and Measurement of Influence," *American Political Science Review*, XLIX (June 1955), pp. 431-451.

possesses a monopoly of sanctions. We shall see, when we come to discuss the "poverty of power," that employees, particularly when they are organized in unions but even when they are not, have a number of effective sanctions at their disposal which they can use to neutralize the power of the employer. Hence the relation is not nearly as one-sided as a narrow view of the legal and formal implications of the employment contract would imply.

2. *Legitimacy*

The motive of legitimacy refers to the tendency of people to do what they feel they "ought" to do. The terms "right" and "wrong" are sometimes defined substantively—"Thou shalt not kill!"—but more often procedurally—"Thou shalt obey the law!" To the extent that people respond to the motive of legitimacy, the acceptance of authority can be secured by legitimizing the right to give orders and the obligation to accept them. "Legitimizing" is used here as a psychological term—the creation of a set of attitudes. The basic psychological mechanisms that create and maintain attitudes of acceptance of legitimate authority are identical with those responsible for the acquisition and internalization of other attitudes.

3. *Social Approval*

Authority is accepted when rejection would incur disapproval from persons whom an individual regards as his "reference group" —a group in which he wants acceptance and approval. Approval and disapproval may properly be regarded as sanctions, but since the reference group is often not the group that can dispose of the other sanctions, the approval-disapproval sanction deserves separate consideration. For the same reason, acceptance of the one authority may entail rejection of the other. Important situations where this occurs will come readily to mind.

There is an important interaction between social approval and the legitimacy motive. When a particular system of authority is accepted as legitimate by members of a group, not only do they tend to accept authority in their own behavior, but they tend also to exhibit disapproval toward members of the group who do not accept it. I would conjecture that it is through this indirect mechanism that the motive of legitimacy obtains its greatest force. The approval mechanism operates as a powerful amplifier to secure compliance with the particular system of authority that the group accepts as legitimate.

4. *Confidence*

Authority is accepted when a decision premise comes from a source that is regarded as technically competent to provide that premise. The authority of a doctor over his patient, of an attorney over his client, are typical examples of the authority of confidence. Both inside and outside organizations much of the authority of the technical specialist derives from this source—particularly the authority that operates upwards and sidewise in the formal organizational hierarchy. The authority of confidence is generally an important part, too, of the authority relation between superiors and subordinates although—as we have just seen—it is not limited to that relation.

Debates about the "proper" definition of the term "authority" usually center around the issue of whether acceptance of behavior premises should be called "authority" regardless of which of the four motivational mechanisms caused the acceptance, or whether the term should be limited to acceptance due to rewards and sanctions, or to the legitimacy motive. We will use here an inclusive definition that embraces all instances of the exercise and acceptance of authority, whatever the motivational base. When it becomes necessary to distinguish among the motivations, we will refer to "authority of sanctions," "authority of legitimacy," "authority of social approval," and "authority of confidence."

AUTHORITY, COERCION, AND MANIPULATION

It is not easy in our society at the present time to use "authority" as a neutral, descriptive term. It transforms itself too easily into "authoritarian," which is more epithet than description. But authority, as I have defined it, is neither good nor bad. It becomes good or bad in particular situations on the basis of our evaluation of the social consequences of its exercise. We regard authority as "coercion" when it rests primarily on sanctions and is used to advance the interests of the party who possesses it against the interests of the other. We regard influence (authority or persuasion) as "manipulation" when it rests on disparity between the parties in their skill and technique of persuasion and negotiation, and when the disparity is used to advance the interests of the stronger against those of the weaker.

The presence or absence of coercion or manipulation—inequality or equality of bargaining power—cannot be assessed simply by the application of an objective measuring rod. In addition to the measurement of the relative balance of authority and influence between parties there is required also an evaluation of the social desirability of this balance.

THE AUTHORITY OF LEGITIMACY

Prior to the present century, serious discussions of authority are to be found principally in the literature of political and legal theory.[4] There are two main themes, although one of them is heard more loudly and frequently than the other.

One theory is concerned with the good man and the good state and treats primarily of the authority of legitimacy. For the most part, the theory is ethical in its goals (if not always in its form), being centrally concerned with locating the fountainheads of legitimacy and defining the jurisdictional boundaries of the various holders of legitimate authority—the state, the church, and the individual.

The second, and weaker, strain in the literature of authority treats primarily of the authority of sanctions. It finds its fullest development in Aristotle's theory of revolutions and in Machiavelli's advice to his prince. I shall have more to say about the "Machiavellian" or "Realpolitik" approaches to the theory of authority in the next section. For the moment, I should like to dwell on what the earlier theory had to say about legitimacy. As I have indicated, the aim of the theory was not to explain the psychological roots of the legitimacy motive, but to decide what authority was legitimate, or "ought to be," and within what limits.

The theories of authority that have come down to us are overwhelmingly conservative—that is to say, almost all of them take for granted that a stable, legitimate social order is essential and

[4] See, for example, William A. Dunning, *A History of Political Theories* (New York: Macmillan, 1920), particularly Vol. III, Chap. 10.

that individuals have a moral obligation to accept, almost always, the legitimate order. Authority is not (or "ought not to be") absolute, however. There is a higher law (divine law or natural law), and when authority is exercised in such an arbitrary and unjust manner as to violate this law, the individual has a right of resistance, and even of revolution—to be exercised, of course, with the greatest prudence and restraint.

Prior to the present century, most discussions of the employment relation—of the relation of master and servant, as the law still calls it—have been very much in this same tradition of legal and political theory. The employment contract, like the social contract, established a relation of legitimate authority of employer over employee. But agreement on this general point settled few issues until there was agreement on the specific terms of the contract: Was it like the one-sided irrevocable pact of Hobbes, or the more cautious, qualified document of Locke? This was a question on which employers and employees seldom saw eye to eye, with the result that the motive of legitimacy could create only the narrower authority that the employee thought he owed the employer, not the broader authority that the employer believed was owed to him.

Authority that is viewed as legitimate is not felt as coercion or manipulation, either by the man who exercises it or by the man who accepts it. Hence, the scientist who wishes to deal with issues of manipulation that are sometimes raised in human relations research must be aware of his own attitudes of legitimacy. In particular, he must understand his own beliefs as to the scope of legitimate authority that is implied by an employment relation. If he regards the area of legitimate authority as narrow, many practices will appear to him coercive or manipulative that would not seem so with a broader criterion of legitimacy.

THE POVERTY OF POWER

When we are confronted with a discrepancy in the views of several parties to an agreement as to what they have agreed to do, it is natural to ask who has, in fact, the power to enforce his viewpoint with sanctions. Modern students of authority—Charles E. Merriam and Chester I. Barnard prominent among them—have observed that the study of enforceability should start with the person who accepts authority rather than the person who seeks to wield it.

The reason is that the behavior authority seeks to control is the behavior of the subordinate, not the behavior of the superior. The acceptance that is secured may be the "I do" of a shotgun wedding, but acceptance there must be. This is not merely a verbal quibble, for it implies that wherever the authority relation exists there must be a mechanism to maintain it, and this mechanism must be efficacious.

In the employment relation, the employer has the sanctions of firing, the lockout, incentive pay, and promotion. But the employee has the sanctions of quitting, the strike, and the slowdown—as well as more subtle means of job control. The strengths of each of these as rewards and sanctions will depend on the state of supply and demand for labor, the degree of organization of labor, the legitimacy or illegitimacy attached by the courts and the state to these several sanctions, and numerous other factors.

When the balance of sanctions is not completely one-sided, however, it is the employer who is faced with the problem of securing acceptance of authority from the employee, and not vice versa. It is this asymmetry that impoverishes the power of sanctions. The employee has at his disposal a whole range of weapons of minimal performance, literal performance, and nonperformance to help him resist attempted exercises of authority that appear to him illegitimate or unwelcome, and hence to enforce his version of the employment bargain.

Under these circumstances, "human relations" may take on very different meanings for the employee and the employer, respectively. The employee wishes to emphasize that when he sells his services he does not sell a commodity. He has feelings and attitudes both about what he is asked to do on the job and how he is asked to do it. If the employer does not enlist his willing acceptance by paying attention to these aspects of the job, the employee may feel justified in demonstrating the employer's inability to compel his acceptance.

When the employer is confronted with the poverty of his power, he too may turn to "human relations." Finding little common ground with the employee as to the legitimate boundaries of his authority, and finding sanctions ineffective as means for motivating acceptance, he may want to find what other motivations there are—and discover the answer in some of the findings of human relations research.

In the problem posed by the two previous paragraphs lie some of the central difficulties of securing acceptance for research in human relations as a neutral scientific activity. I do not mean to assert that human relations research always *has* been entirely neutral, but that even if it had, it would have a hard time convincing the parties to the employment contract that it was so. Let us look at what some human relations research has had to say about the authority concept.

THE SUPERIORITY OF "DEMOCRACY"

Perhaps I should indicate what I am including in the term "human relations research." Broadly, I mean research that is directed at understanding the motivations and behaviors of humans in groups; somewhat more narrowly, I mean research on human behavior in the industrial setting.

There is, of course, no official body of "human relations" doctrine. On the other hand, there is a considerable measure of agreement among the principal investigators about several central generalizations. One such generalization is the *participation hypothesis*: to bring about change in behavior in an organization and to get effective acceptance of new practices, it is necessary to secure the active participation in the decision of those whose behavior will be affected by the change.

A second generalization is the *social approval hypothesis*: the most powerful sanction influencing an individual employee is the approval and disapproval of the other members of his work group.

An employer who experiences the poverty of power and finds the authority of legitimacy and sanctions inadequate to his managerial tasks may seek to enlist the mechanisms of participation and social approval as means of persuasion and as additional motivations for the acceptance of authority.[5] He is likely to be successful to the extent that the several parties to the employment contract *perceive* their goals to be more or less parallel.

Let us consider first the social approval hypothesis. I have stated the hypothesis in a weaker form than one usually finds in the literature. The statement often is that increase in social cohesion of the work group will increase the productivity of the employee. Evidence from studies of productivity and morale does not bear out this

[5] On this whole topic see Wilbert E. Moore, *Industrial Relations and the Social Order* (Rev. ed.; New York: Macmillan, 1951), Chaps. 7 and 8.

stronger hypothesis with any consistency. The reason is that there will be a positive correlation between productivity and morale only to the extent that goals approved by the work group are consistent with goals of management. Both reason and empirical evidence generally support this more qualified statement.

It is also clear why the participation mechanism is useful to the employer only under the assumption of substantial parallelism of interests. The employer can tolerate genuine participation in decision-making only when he believes that reasonable men, knowing the relevant facts and thinking through the problem, will reach a decision that is generally consistent with *his* goals and interests in the situation. This requires that they must, at least in part, share those goals and interests or have parallel ones. Participation can bolster the authority of confidence and can supplement authority with persuasion, but it can do these things only to the extent that the parties perceive themselves as working toward common goals.

Pioneer research in human relations has been much criticized for the enthusiasm with which it advocated participation in decision-making and encouragement of group cohesion as solutions for the human problems of the workplace. The basis for that criticism has been sketched in the preceding paragraphs. The error arose because it was assumed implicitly that there was an underlying community of goals between employer and employees and because this assumption was never made explicit or subjected to careful empirical examination.

Because symptoms of industrial strife are so easily and commonly observed, a lack of good faith has sometimes been charged against persons who have made the implicit assumption of community of goals in interpreting their research findings, and the adjective "manipulative" has been applied to human relations techniques. I have no way of knowing whether employers have accepted and attempted to apply the findings of human relations research in good or in bad faith. But I think it is easy enough to explain how a reasonable man, even in the face of evidence of industrial strife, still could make the assumption of community of goals.

It has been an overwhelmingly prevalent ideology in this country that the way to get more pie is to bake a larger one, not to quarrel about the slicing of the smaller one. (I am not concerned with the truth of the statement, but with the widespread belief in it.) How could an employer reconcile his acceptance of this tenet, and his belief that his employees accepted it, with their observable resistance to his authority—his "managerial prerogatives"?

1. He could suppose that he had misjudged their goals—that they were interested not merely in the pay envelope but also in satisfactions, social and otherwise, associated directly with the job.

2. He could suppose that they did not have a complete enough understanding of the advantages to them (through the increased size of the pie) of the action he was proposing.

If the employer adopted the first line of interpretation, he would likely have become, a generation ago, a highly paternalistic employer, or, today, an enthusiastic "human relator." If the employer adopted the second line of interpretation, he would seek, via the participation mechanism, to supplant the employees' "sentiments" with his own "logic." In all these cases the outcome would depend not only on what he did, but on how his employees interpreted his actions.

We see that the findings of human relations research, *if* they are combined explicitly with the assumption of community of goals, can be used to show a deep-lying consistency between good and effective managerial practices, on the one hand, and the generally accepted values of our culture on the other:

1. Employer and employee have the common goal of creating a larger product that will be shared not only between them, but with the consumer and the investor as well.

2. Excessive reliance on formal authority and the authority derivable from sanctions is not an effective way of producing this larger product. Hence there is no conflict of good managerial practice with the democratic and anti-authoritarian values of our culture.

3. The pleasant workplace is the productive workplace. Hence there is no conflict of good managerial practice with the desires of employees to derive satisfactions from their jobs and from social activity connected with their work.

EFFICIENCY OR SATISFACTION

Each of the three main tenets of the doctrine sketched in the preceding section has been the subject of critical re-examination. The question of the size of the pie and who shares it is beyond the scope of the present essay—it would lead us over the whole area of industrial relations, anti-trust policy, government-business relations, and what not. Our concern will be with the other two issues, which we will find it convenient to label "authority or democracy" and "efficiency or satisfaction," respectively.

The doctrine has not gone unchallenged that "democratic" administration—administration that depends heavily upon participation in decisions and that does not brandish its formal authority—is the most effective administration. Without attempting to survey the literature in detail, one might note particularly the work of Barnard, Homans, and Argyris in re-examining the functions of status differentials in organizations and in challenging the notion that a large-scale organization can or should be egalitarian.

The situation with respect to efficiency and satisfaction is somewhat more complicated. Early proponents of scientific management adopted a fairly narrow, almost physiological, point of view; emphasized short-run efficiency through specialization; and pretty well neglected the subtler motivational aspects of the problem—including the satisfactions of the worker *on the job*. Early human relations research directed attention to the worker's job satisfactions and the long-run feedback of these upon performance; it undoubtedly swung the pendulum too far in assuming that if job satisfactions were handled, efficiency would take care of itself. More recent studies—e.g., the work of Bavelas and Leavitt with small laboratory "organizations"—re-emphasize the short-run conflict between work arrangements that are physiologically efficient and those that produce satisfaction, and cast doubt on the thesis that maintenance of an appropriate level of satisfaction will automatically assure a high level of productive efficiency.

The consequences of taking the middle ground with respect to either of these issues—authority v. democracy or efficiency v. satisfaction—do not seem to me particularly disturbing. We need simply to accept the fact that designing organizations, like designing the buildings that house them, is a rather complex activity and that organization design, like architecture, is a process of continual compromise in which we are always deciding how we shall divide our limited budget between more floor space and more attractive furnishings.

As long as these compromises have to be made, we must expect that employers and employees will often disagree as to the weights to be assigned to conflicting goals. What these weights should be is a matter to be settled by bargaining, not by scientific evidence. Researchers in human relations have perhaps not always been clear where scientific evidence ended and their own values began, and they have perhaps tended at times to gloss over or to rationalize away genuine conflict of interest. There can be little doubt, however, that two decades of research in this field have made enormous contributions to our understanding of attitudes toward authority in our culture and of the motivations for accepting or rejecting it.

IN CONCLUSION

Management involves a combination of persuasion and the exercise of authority. It has to operate within a context that is perceived as involving both conflicting and parallel interests. Authority that rests solely or largely on sanctions is inadequate to the tasks of management, for the sanctions do not all lie on one side of the employment relation and the employee has many means of defending himself from the manager's attempts to enforce his authority.

Managerial authority may seek its second support in the mechanism of legitimacy, but this support extends only to the limits of the employees' acceptance of legitimacy. If authority is to extend beyond these limits, it must depend on other mechanisms—upon social approval and on confidence.

Much contemporary human relations research may be interpreted as seeking to enlarge the means for motivating members of organizations toward the acceptance of organization goals and of organization authority. The research has resulted in increased emphasis upon the mechanisms of persuasion, social approval, and confidence. Employee participation in decision-making and the strengthening of work-group influence over individual employees have been proposed as two important organizational techniques to this end.

The more recent work along these lines has shown, however, that authority based on social approval and confidence depends heavily upon perceived parallelism of interest between employers and employees. We have had to moderate the optimism of some of the early human relations research which took that parallelism for granted and equated conflict with ignorance or lack of skill in human relations. Our present view is more balanced—at the expense of being more complex and less easily applied. In a world in which there was always a complete conflict of interests—in which all games were zero-sum—the terms "authority," "power," "coercion," and "manipulation" would be used almost synonymously. In such a world authority would extend only as far as the club could reach that enforced it, and the only function of knowledge of human behavior would be to give the party who possessed it power to manipulate. All bargains would be necessitous.

Clearly, most of us do not view the world in quite this way. We recognize areas of competition, but we do not regard these areas as coterminous with the whole of social life, nor the competition as lawless. Hence, we distinguish between an authority relation—which seems to us an acceptable and frequently useful pattern of social behavior—and a coercive or manipulative relationship, of which we disapprove. The problem of authority is one of the central issues that is always present, whether acknowledged or not, at the bargaining table. As management representatives and union leaders gain a deeper understanding of this problem they will be prepared increasingly to search for ways of enlisting the authority of legitimacy, of social approval, and of confidence in the pursuit of goals that employer and employee can both accept.

COMMENTARY ON MR. SIMON'S CHAPTER

BY SOLOMON BARKIN
Textile Workers Union of America

Human relations research originated as an inquiry into management's ability to control workers' output by manipulating the physical environment. Recognizing the limitations of this approach, investigators offered a new approach through manipulation of the human work group. Thereafter, practitioners of the human relations school sought new devices for controlling worker groups. But they worked against the tide. Unionism had taken hold and spread broadly throughout American industry during the thirties and the war and early postwar period. Failing to stem this tide, personnel and industrial relations men pressed academicians to formulate more refined techniques for overcoming employee resistance and eliciting employee cooperation with management.

As research progressed, more objective investigators came to a parting of the ways with management's singular objective. They concluded that manipulative and communication devices could not, by themselves, overcome real differences in interest existing between employers and employees. They joined the current movement for studying industrial peace. Employer-employee cooperation, they found, had to be built upon recognition of workers' independent interests and the need of accommodating workers and employers to each other's goals. Knowledge of human relations can help both parties come to terms with the realities of our industrial society.

Human relations analysts, like industrial relations men and labor economists, have come to realize that, despite the many common interests, employers and workers have different and competitive goals in a free economic society. The pursuit of these logics is essential to a democratic capitalistic economy. Our political democracy has encouraged labor organizations to equalize the bargaining power of workers and employers. The division between worker and employer is due not to perversity nor to ignorance but to essentially contrasting objectives. Sound industrial relations programs must be built upon acceptance of these differences and not on a myth of an all-pervading identity of interest.

Traditional human relations research has hitherto supported the older and increasingly obsolete theory that employees will wholeheartedly adopt the employer system of logics. The reason for this preoccupation is to be found in the origins of the discipline. It began under management's auspices in the era of welfare capitalism. Management took it over most avidly in postwar years when it sought new ways to avoid unions or at least to put them in their place as adjuncts to the enterprises rather than co-equals within them.

The present chapter reveals that academic research has progressed well beyond this position. Small groups and communication techniques are by themselves no certain way to win over workers. Employees, in fact, use them to promote their own interests and, if necessary, subvert management's.

Traditional human relations philosophy stressed the effectiveness of manipulative techniques to gain workers' support. What employers cannot achieve through economic incentives or sanctions, they can attain through propaganda devices. Instead of pursuing the workers' own channels of communication, formalized most among organized workers but also discernible among the unorganized, management approaches them directly through its own representatives. The aim is not to secure consideration of issues by workers in terms of their self-interest in a setting free of coercive influences. Management rather seeks acceptance of its objectives by workers in a controlled atmosphere. By accepting such ascendency for employer goals, the worker is diverted from independent influences and a frank evaluation of the proposals in terms of respective management and worker objectives. He will then accept management's right and competency to give direct orders and the superiority of its value system.

Techniques of manipulation, as with all propaganda, will vary, but the elements remain similar. They will include excessive simplification of issues, omission of essential facts, use of ambiguous language, images, and data, and exploitation of prestige personalities to reinforce the message. Threats and sanctions will, at times, be used to support or hasten acceptance of the message.

Participation in management-controlled meetings or captive audiences is not democracy, no matter how simulated the forms may be. It allows for little free discussion or decision-making. The threat of superior economic force is ever present and sufficient to cow workers into subordinating or sublimating their own values and thoughts. The precedures allow for "brainwashing" and the use of suggestion to impose management's views. In its most successful development, workers will accept management's premises and work out rationalizations to explain their submission in face of the obvious conflict with their own interests.

Personnel and industrial relations men and industrial engineers continue to stress the value of manipulative efforts in selling their proposals. Administrators are so taken with this attitude that when programs either falter or fail, they are sure it is merely because workers were incorrectly approached.

These are the arts of seduction of free humans, not the ways of debate with equals. The insidiousness of the arts of the propagandist is widely recognized. In the free world, the individual is often protected through competition of ideas. But at his place of employment, the worker needs his own organization to help him pierce the barrage of propaganda and evaluate freely management's goals and policies.

The use of ambiguous and mellifluous words such as "human relations" to describe these practices compounds the villainy of the deception. It takes close study and time to recognize the malignant purposes and unrealistic assumptions of such a "human relations" approach.

Students of the science of "human relations" must discharge a special debt to the industrial world and clearly proclaim, as Mr. Simon does, that differences in labor and management interests must be recognized. Management's traditional human relations approach does not advance sound industrial relations. At a minimum, it delays them; at its worst, it helps maintain management's domination of our working population.

A sound system of industrial relations requires the maintenance of an independent organization of workers. With the aid and protection of these unions, workers can freely consider management's objectives and proposals in terms of their own self-interest as well as their common purposes, and negotiate agreements on terms of employment. Free collective bargaining eliminates the need for manipulative devices. Agreements define management's areas of legitimate authority and competence and the proper use of sanctions. Human relations research should guide in group formation and direction, improve communication through normal channels, and point the way to better adaption of the job environment, schedule, and demands to humans.

· VIII ·

MANAGEMENT AND UNION ORGANIZATIONS: AN ANALYTICAL COMPARISON

BY WILBERT E. MOORE
Princeton University

Within the wide range of human groups and patterns of action, management and union organizations stand in an otherwise surprising proximity. Both are deliberately created, with specific and limited objectives. Members are recruited by a formal act of "joining." Membership involves specific rights and duties, at least partially codified in formal rules and procedures. Although both may be viewed as structures of positions and roles, with considerable continuity in the face of turnover of particular occupants, membership at a given time may be fairly readily identified. Since neither is in principle an encompassing or "totalitarian" organization in its effects on members' lives and activities, each is faced with the possibility of competing loyalties and claims on such scarce resources as time, and of consequent "role conflicts" for the individual participant.

This cursory statement of common features can be partially summarized by sociological shorthand. Despite many and important differences, management and union organizations belong to a common general type of human aggregation. Both are *associations,* as distinct from communities, primary groups, crowds, or publics.

Membership in both organizations is directly related to position in the productive system. The type of productive system in which they appear is one that differentiates jobs or occupations from other roles, and productive organizations from other membership groups (such as the kinship system or community).

ORGANIZATIONAL TYPE

Despite the fact that both management and union organizations may be called *associations,* further classification leads to a sharp differentiation in taxonomic location. In terms of structure, management belongs to the sub-class of *administrative organizations* and the union to the sub-class of *voluntary associations.* Many of the characteristics of each, as well as some of the problems of their mutual relations, stem from these basic structural categories.

Management as an Administrative Organization

Managerial organization is fundamentally bureaucratic in its non-derogatory sense. That is, it shares with agencies of the modern state and many educational and welfare organizations various characteristic modes of internal differentiation, operating procedures, and standardized solutions to recurrent problems.

As a group, the administrative organization has a clear-cut criterion of membership, for this comprises the individual's job and thus typically his livelihood. Whatever other bonds or types of relationship the individual has as a consequence of his employment, or whatever the range of his actual "need-satisfactions" that are thereby fulfilled, he has a minimally essential financial relation to the organization. This is to say that it is a "work" organization. But this clear criterion of membership also is a principal means whereby an individual's job is related to other social activities and obligations, and a ready means of rewarding or symbolizing position with the organization.

The administrative organization has a marked internal heterogeneity. For the accomplishment of its objectives it places extensive reliance on specialization and division of labor. In a sense, therefore, the collective results are an operational by-product of individual and "team" activities.

The results do not emerge solely from specialization among

equals, however. One of the most commonly noted features of administrative organization is its hierarchical structure—its coordination of specialized activities through a system of graded authority.

All this presupposes an extended and indirect system of communication, which carries orders and directives, information relevant to decisions, and information on "current state" including confirmation that the communicative net is still operating. For this net to operate it is not necessary for everyone to understand every communication or have a common "definition of the situation." This is manifestly impossible with elaborate technical specialization. The system does require links, translators, and interpreters; this requirement tends to reinforce authoritative coordination which also discourages "lateral" communication.

The member of the administrative "group" thus has a *financial,* a *technical* or occupational, a *political* (in the sense of relative power), and a *communicative* relation to the organization. He may also have an ideological commitment to the objectives of the organization and its codes or the characteristic beliefs of members. He may have psychological commitments to his job that go beyond its financial rewards. He may also have various social relations with other members at the workplace. These are not, in the pure case, required, however. For the relations are essentially between positions or functions. The interdependence that specialization requires theoretically makes each position critical or indispensable, although its particular occupant is not.

The administrative organization may also be viewed as a normative system. In common with all associations its announced objectives are specific, limited, and, in principle, graded. To achieve these objectives there is a normatively prescribed set of activities and a prescribed mode of orientation toward decisions and problems. That is, there is an expectation of *rational* use of organizational resources (including notably personnel). Because everyone is now sensitized to the existence of irrational and nonrational motivation, there has been a tendency to understate the importance of "institutionalized" rationality. That is, problems are expected to be resolved by fact and logic, and not simply by tradition or whimsical preference. This austere expectation does in practice get glossed over as well as flagrantly violated, but its importance remains.

"Bureaucracy" is generally, and properly, associated with a multiplicity of detailed rules. Although operating codes are often exasperating to the outsider and indeed permit excessive involvement in forms ritualistically followed, the general function of such rules is to assure predictability of behavior in highly complex relations. Specifically, the rules serve to allocate activities according to spheres of competence, including limits on the exercise of authority; allocate personnel according to technical merit; depersonalize relationships in view of potential social heterogeneity and of turnover in particular offices and in membership generally.

A critical question in comparing management and union organization is the source of authority. The actual "representatives" of management in relations with the union derive their authority by "delegation" and are thus responsible "up the line" and not "down the line," although technical specialization makes likely some sphere of autonomy on procedures and details if not on general results. The more important problem, however, is whence comes the authority of top executives. The traditional answer in the legal institutions of capitalism has been, "from the owners." This answer is subject to considerable skepticism, increasingly expressed, not only because of the common "separation of ownership and management" but also because management in fact is in some sense also responsible to other groups and interests: suppliers, consumers, governmental rules and agencies, and employees. Thus the management of a modern industrial corporation operates in a somewhat cloudy atmosphere with respect to its authority and responsibilities, the interests represented, and how those interests make themselves felt.

The Union as a Voluntary Association

The basic type and form of union organization puts it in a class with clubs, fraternal orders, religious denominations, and a tremendous range of "interest groups." Although the structural consequences are not otherwise unimportant, this basic type remains even if the membership is in fact involuntary in some degree. At most this presumably entails a reluctant and coerced minority, but does not mean complete abandonment of democratic forms and procedures.

A more serious reservation on the legitimacy of the classification is the administrative "superstructure" of union organizations, at least at the national level. Here the union also is a bureaucracy, with some characteristics very similar to those of management and other work organizations. The union, too, provides a direct livelihood for its administrative staff, specializes functions, coordinates by authority, and relies on a complex communicative network. Relationships are necessarily formalized and routinized, with operating codes and rules of conduct.

The differences in management and union administrative organization are instructive. Union organization typically has much less technical specialization than does management. (Size, however, must be taken into account, as a large national union may have a glittering array of technical talent as compared with a small independent firm.) This smaller development of "staff" functions derives from factors partly intrinsic, partly historical. As compared with management, the union generally has a narrower range of functions and interests for which advanced technical information is required. It has, moreover, generally smaller resources for staff expansion, in view of its dependence upon dues and fees for support. "Slush funds" of unions are, relative to size, generally smaller than disposable resources of corporations.

The small, but growing, utilization of technical and professional services by unions also has other sources. Because the union is, or has been, a "conflict" organization with strong political and emotional overtones in internal policy, there has been a heavy reliance on a leadership of experience and an assumption of the "universal competence" of that leadership. The first moves toward staff specialization have been close to "window dressing," that is, have involved external relations with governmental organs and the courts, with the "public," or with management when technical problems of pensions or, more rarely, job specifications have been argued. The use of a technical staff in the formation of internal policy is recent and somewhat rare, and the staff specialist of whatever variety is likely to have a more circumscribed sphere of autonomy or functional authority than his management counterpart.

The norm of rationality is probably less firmly established in unions than in corporations. Again, this is partly because of the importance of ideology in a conflict group, partly because of the importance of the *political* support of the rank and file. Fact and logic remain important in union action, however, and the apparent differences are more in objectives and specific means than in abandonment of national conduct by unions. Questions of loyalty tend to be more acutely emphasized among union administrators than among managers. This expected loyalty is not simply ideological (identification with the union) but often personal with respect to the top leadership. In this as in other respects unions bear a stronger resemblance to political than to business administrations.

A final contrast between management and union administrative organization leads directly to the characteristics of unions as "voluntary associations." This difference is the source of authority. The particular union staff officer may be accountable to his administrative superior as in any bureaucratic administration. The entire administrative organization, through the elected executives at the top, is ultimately accountable to the membership of the union as a whole. As compared with corporate executives, the formal accountabilities of union leaders are clear and unambiguous. The people to be satisfied in terms of the exercise of authority are the rank and file members.

The standard voluntary association has a constitution and bylaws, elected officers, regular and special committees, periodic meetings, and an endemic apathy on the part of many members. Unions typically share these organizational features.

In structural terms, union organization below the administrative level may be said to comprise two crudely distinguishable sectors—the active center and the passive periphery. The former normally includes officers and committee chairmen and some members (who are probably, as "good organization people," past or future officers and committeemen). Passivity or apathy is of course a matter of degree, and of variable issues and circumstances, but the probability is high that it characterizes most members most of the time. Like management, but for quite different reasons, the union is typically under effective minority control. This in turn accounts for the possibility that an ideologically cohesive minority may control a union whose members are in vast majority not sympathetic to the ideology.

Aside from salaried officials, the union member is a dues-payer, an officer or part of the potential electorate, and a potential "participant" in whatever range of activities or services the union provides. If the union acts solely or primarily as an economic bargaining agency, the member *may* regard the union as a "commodity" (a service purchased with dues). If it also acts as an educational, recreational, and political organization, he may regard it as something of a "community." These links between the member and the organization are somewhat analogous to those prevailing in the managerial structure. They are not the same, and the differences derive from the basic dissimilarity in organizational types.

PROBLEMS OF INTERNAL RELATIONS

Neither management nor union can safely assume that organizational objectives and individual ends coincide, nor is this assumption required for organization success in a safe and stable environment and with adequate allocation of tasks. Success then only requires that whatever rewards the individual derives from his performance remain adequate to assure that performance, which in turn is a means to group goals. Management may rely on "bribed interdependence" and the union on "bribed participation." The assumptions noted, however, are theoretical and not actual. Both organizations face persistent problems of internal cohesion and of loyalty to objectives. Even if the two are not competing with each other for loyalty of common members, as limited-interest associations they must compete with or adjust to the total range of human aspirations and social affiliations. The allegiance of members is always partial and therefore somewhat problematical.

Conflict and Cooperation Within Management

Behind the appearance of the administrative organization as a complex but efficient social machine lie many actual and potential points of tension and conflict, of failure and duplication, of minimal performance and exaggerated successes. Some of these departures from the model are by-products of piecemeal change, others arise from the intrusion of perfectly "normal" but specifically disruptive human interests, and others seem inherent in the nature of the organization itself.

Changes in size, products, staff services, and even in personnel introduce major or minor crises in administrative organizations.

These changes are likely to raise questions of adequate integration and communication, of jurisdiction, and occasionally even of major policies.

The relation of the individual to the organization is a potential source of tension, if not of group conflict. Every bureaucratic organization is faced with at least three standard tendencies: *lethargy* (limits on performance), *corruption* (substitution of individual for organizational goals), and *technicism* (a converting of prescribed means into ends and ritualistic adherence to them). In a sense, all of these involve questions of loyalty as well as efficiency.

Potential cleavages within management also stem from some inherent organizational problems. Perhaps the most notable of these problems is the relation between *amount* and *kind* of authority. In a crude way this may be equated with the ubiquitous line-staff conflict, but the latter has other sources as well. There are tensions between the lay administrator and the expert subordinate, between those whose primary loyalty is to the organization or their administrative superiors and those whose loyalty is to the occupation or their professional colleagues, between persons with previous broad responsibilities and those representing new specialized functions. In each case these potential cleavages tend to demarcate line and staff, and in each the question of authority or sphere of competence is at least indirectly involved.

Other organizational sources or opportunities for conflict include disputes over priorities in ultimate objectives, disputes over appropriate means, and, notably, competing claims on such scarce resources as the annual budget (but also power, influence, prestige).

Cooperation within management is accordingly not automatic, nor simply a question of "leadership." It depends not only upon such structural devices as communicative nets and clear-cut jurisdictions, but also upon adequate motivation, reduction of cross-pressures or role conflicts, and, perhaps, development of positive organizational loyalties. Collective loyalty in a highly heterogeneous organization is most likely to be produced by external threat or conflict, and this in turn may undermine the otherwise efficient norm of rationality by appeals to sentiment, traditional rights or prerogatives, and spurious claims to a monopoly of wisdom and justice.

A brief comment should be added concerning "informal" organization. This hazy concept has come to represent a residual category: all actions and relations not represented in charts and manuals of procedure. On close inspection this residue will be found to include actions necessary to the operation of the organization and accomplishment of objectives, but not specified in rules because of the impossibility of complete planning or because of the inefficiency of prescribed procedures. Other actions will represent accumulated precedent, which is binding though unwritten. Illustrations of informal organization commonly refer to the "enrichment" of relations through the addition of bases and manners of interaction beyond (or even instead of) those technically required. Here again, the organization or pattern of action that is informal arises from some of the characteristics of work organizations themselves. They provide continuous, face-to-face contact among limited aggregates of people and thus make virtually certain extensive personal involvement in interaction. It should be emphasized, however, that such groups or patterns of communication exist within and partially derive from "formal" organizations. Theoretical approaches that assume that such "primary groups" (which they usually are not) constitute the building blocks of industrial organizations have extremely limited utility for predicting behavior within management or administrative organizations generally.

Management has attempted to utilize informal organization by such devices as group discussion and decision. These devices, intended both as a part of the system of communication and as a way of increasing the individual's sense of worth and participation, thus formalize part of what goes on anyway, but never all of it.

Conflict and Cooperation Within the Union

The formal structure of unions, unlike that of management, assumes internal disagreement. It is conflict within management that requires explanation; it is consensus within the union. As a democratic organization, the union provides procedures for conducting disputes (parliamentary forms) and for their resolution (majority vote). The facts of union operation depart somewhat from these norms. It is indeed not even clear that the democratic *norm* is always accepted in all its implications in union organization, as a dispute over issues or even presentation of a rival slate of officers is commonly referred to as "factionalism."

The administrative structure of national unions falls heir to many of the same problems that beset management. Union administrations are, however, usually smaller and their members more homogeneous in background and, possibly, in ideology. Despite these advantages in maintaining administrative harmony, the decisional processes in determining the range and priority of objectives are complicated not only by considerable uncertainty as to just what these objectives are at a specific time, but also by the probable existence of diversity of interests and views at lower organizational levels. Thus within the union administrative group there is potential conflict over objectives and strategies in dealing with, say, management and also in dealing with the union membership.

Effective union democracy is more likely to appear at the local level. National union policies may get a local and acrimonious airing, and the behavior of local officers in handling grievances may be criticized, but it is particularly in industrial unions that a more pervasive source of dissension appears. Emphasis on common employee status as a criterion of union membership does not remove genuine differences in occupational interests. Neither managerial nor union policies will uniformly affect all occupations equally or even in the same direction. In any given instance a particular occupational group may be outvoted. In the long run dissidence may accumulate, and the union may actually split into separate units. An effective grievance procedure not only serves to keep the union an active agent for the workers between contracts but also helps quiet discontented minorities within the union.

Aside from the very real difficulty of maintaining a strong union administration with democratic controls, the major reason the unions attempt to minimize debate and achieve an apparent consensus is the presumed necessity of presenting a united front before management and the public. The formal structure of unions is primarily shaped by that objective. The utility of conflict for achieving cohesion and loyalty is the same in this as in any other group. Its cost may well be an effective suppression of discussion and the loss of some distinctive features of the voluntary association including the opportunity of the individual to help shape organizational policy.

The line of argument to this point suggests a kind of paradox in union behavior. With external conflict democratic participation may be considered impossible; with peace it may be unnecessary. In other words, apathy as measured by nonattendance at meetings or nonparticipation in discussion may indicate satisfaction rather than alienation. Union leaders may be ambivalent about increasing participation. Ideologically they may be committed to strong and vigorous democracy, as well as the maintenance of morale for bargaining strength. As practical politicians they may welcome the freedom of action and security of tenure permitted by an apathetic membership.

The importance of the union for a member may not be confined to formal meetings and out-of-hours activities, or its performance as a periodic bargaining agent. Its mere existence as an avenue of protest and protection may serve to give the worker a new sense of importance and the erect posture of something like a human being.

CONCLUDING COMMENTS

The way each organization influences and is influenced by its significant setting, including notably the other organization, has been left out of account in this discussion. It is perhaps sufficient to note that management's external orientation is multisided or multidirectional. Its attempt to balance, predict, or possibly control various external interests somewhat limits its organizational flexibility and the commitment of its resources for dealing with the union. The union, although perhaps engaged in periodic political activity, public relations, community services, or interunion rivalry, is much more likely to be able to shape and change its organization and procedures for the primary aims of successful bargaining.

The comparison attempted here has been based upon "standard" forms and generalized characteristics. This neglects wide empirical variations. It cannot be assumed, moreover, that the range of empirical variation in structures exhausts the theoretical range. Such an assumption could only rest on the further assumption that past organizational evolution and deliberate invention have covered all possibilities. Both management and unions probably waste intelligence and experience at lower, and possibly at all, organizational levels. Neither has effectively resolved the conflict between common organizational and diverse individual or group (including occupational) interests and values. The line between "management" and "labor" commonly goes unchallenged, but has scant theoretical basis. It may have less as skill levels and man-machine relations change. It is possible to imagine a situation in which all industrial occupations and administrative levels have formal representation of their interests, with *ad hoc* or loose continuing organizations for their united interests and semiautonomous units with shifting coalitions for their special interests. This would serve to increase the avenues for representation and protest. It is also possible to imagine such close integration of structures through cooperation or "joint determination" that wherever the individual turns for redress of grievances he sees the same faces. Theory can produce nightmares, too.

· IX ·

WORK GROUP BEHAVIOR AND THE LARGER ORGANIZATION*

BY LEONARD R. SAYLES
Columbia University

The individual's most immediate and meaningful experiences of work are obtained in the context of the work group and his work associates. The larger organization is experienced by indirection, but membership in the small group contributes directly to the shaping of attitudes and behavior toward the entire world of work. For this reason of potency, therefore, the contribution of the small group to the total organization has been a subject of substantial research by those interested in human relations in industry.

CONCEPTIONS OF THE WORK GROUP

As Whyte observes, the individual is *not* a member of a single group within a larger structure.[1] Rather, he typically interacts in a variety of settings within the organization. It is the task of the researcher to identify those interaction patterns which are focused and concentrated so that it is reasonable to speak of a "group."

* A substantial portion of the material included is from a study by the author sponsored by the Bureau of Industrial Relations of the University of Michigan on the relationship of work group behavior to technological and organizational factors. Our major emphasis is on industrial work groups, although examples will be drawn from other work settings.

[1] William F. Whyte, "Small Groups in Large Organizations," in *Social Psychology at the Crossroads*, John Rohrer and Muzafer Sherif, eds. (New York: Harper, 1951), pp. 303-304.

If we follow all the members of the organization through their hours on the job, or find some "high" vantage point and observe the total of all interactions, we are likely to be impressed with this proliferation of memberships. Most apparent is membership, except for that unique individual, the president, in some *command group;* that is, the employee shares a common supervisor with a number of colleagues. Distinguishable from this group, but closely related, is a *functional* or *task group*—those employees who must collaborate in some fashion if the work task defined by the organization is to be accomplished. In fact, both of these groups are rather well defined by the larger organization, and the group typically retains those boundaries.

However, there are two other kinds of clusterings that tend to overlap and penetrate the organization in unexpected ways. They are not defined by the formal organization and are often included under the general term, informal organization. One has received much attention from researchers: the *friendship clique.* The other is less well studied, but equally important. That is the *interest group.* This is comprised of those employees who share a common economic interest and seek to gain some objective relating to the larger organization.

Memberships in these groups are not exclusive; often they will overlap considerably. However, the motivations of the members, and, more important, their behavior, are distinctive; and we have no reason to believe that the boundaries will be perfectly coincident.

The Command Group

Perhaps the most obvious kind of small group in the large organization is composed of the supervisor and his immediate subordinates. As Jacques observes, the entire organization is composed of interconnected *command groups,* the subordinates in one group being the superiors in their own command group, with the exception of the first level.[2] While we might expect that research would have emphasized this unit of the organization, if we exclude the manifold studies of leadership styles dealt with elsewhere in this volume, there are relatively few systematic explorations of the relationship between the leader and his subordinates as a group, as individuals,

[2] Elliot Jacques, *The Changing Culture of a Factory* (New York: Dryden Press, 1952), pp. 273-297.

and among the subordinates themselves. Jacques' volume is a notable exception.[3] His examination of the command group has a strong psychiatric flavor. He stresses the leader's ambivalence: his *authority* over his subordinates and *dependence* upon them, his sense of isolation, the problem of integrating pair relationships (leader and individual subordinates) with cohesiveness among subordinates, and the mixed feelings of the subordinates as a group who find the leader both expendable and indispensable (one to be protected or exposed?).

The Friendship Clique

This has been conceived as the elementary building block of human organization. As Mayo writes, "Man's desire to be continuously associated with his fellows is a strong, if not the strongest human characteristic."[4]

At the workplace we find a multitude of friendship groups representing the diverse interests of the workers placed there by the organization. The boundaries of these clusterings appear to reflect the employees' off-the-job interests and associations or previous work experience. Age, ethnic background, outside activities, sex, marital status, and so on, comprise the mortar that binds the clique together.

The friendship group has emerged as the agency which welds the individual to the organization. Loyalty, even attachment, to the total organization with its impersonality, extended hierarchy, and social distance becomes ambiguous. However, attachment to the immediate and easily perceived face-to-face group is the predominant reality of organization experience. For the individual it provides a source of personal security in an impersonal environment.

Where cliques are largely nonexistent, as in the rapidly expanding aircraft plants of California, turnover can be enormous. The

[3] There are two other noteworthy recent exceptions. Argyris devotes a small volume to the relationship between a plant manager in a medium-sized factory and his immediate subordinates. (Chris Argyris, *Executive Leadership* [New York: Harper, 1954]). Two researchers at the Harvard Business School provide us with a very revealing study of the day-to-day changes in the relationship between a first-line supervisor and assembly-line girls during a period of technological changes—Harriet Ronken and Paul Lawrence, *Administering Changes* (Boston: Graduate School of Business Administration, Harvard University, 1952).

[4] Elton Mayo, *Social Problems of an Industrial Civilization* (Boston: Graduate School of Business Administration, Harvard University, 1945), p. 111.

presumption is that stable social groups take time to crystallize; during the period of formation many potential members will leave voluntarily because they do not find an established unit with which they can affiliate. This in turn inhibits the formation of permanent groups; the process is self-defeating.

Thus Lombard and Mayo conclude that the naive administrator who seeks to break up these cliques because of the inefficiency and wasted motion of the purely social activities involved is actually doing a disservice to the organization.[5] In fact, they find that it takes skillful leadership to encourage their formation, at least in organizations undergoing rapid expansion. A recent well-received text[6] in the field of public administration comes out strongly on the side of encouraging on-the-job social life, concluding that production increased when social conversation was allowed. However, a study employing methods of precise interaction observation is unique in casting some doubts as to the positive correlation between social interaction and productivity.[7]

More serious criticism of the universal efficacy of friendship cliques, however, involves considerations of personality and work structure differences. A study of "rate busters" disclosed a significant majority who were indifferent to, if not hostile to, the social groupings they found on the job.[8]

A recent examination of British longshoremen finds that approximately half of the longshoremen on the docks studied have consciously avoided social entanglements of work group membership. Given an opportunity to join semipermanent gangs, they prefer random work assignments that leave them free to come and go at will, with no group responsibility.[9]

Formation of social groups also appears to be a function of the

[5] Elton Mayo and George F. Lombard, *Teamwork and Labor Turnover in the Aircraft Industry of Southern California* (Boston: Graduate School of Business Administration, Harvard University, 1940).

[6] Herbert Simon, Donald Smithburg, and Victor Thompson, *Public Administration* (New York: Knopf, 1950), pp. 113-114.

[7] A. B. Horsfall and Conrad Arensberg, "Teamwork and Productivity in a Shoe Factory," *Human Organization*, VIII (Winter 1949), pp. 21 ff.

[8] These men tended to have a rural background emphasizing individualism. Orvis Collins and Donald Roy, "Restriction of Output and Social Cleavage in Industry," *Applied Anthropology*, V (Summer 1946), pp. 1-14.

[9] University of Liverpool, *The Dock Worker* (Liverpool: University Press of Liverpool, 1954), pp. 61 ff.

structure of the work situation itself. Argyris, in his Bank study, finds that incidence of informal social groupings among tellers is less than for bank employees who have less interaction with customers.[10] This conclusion would confirm a basic hypothesis of Chapple, that individuals seek some equilibrium in their rate and range of interaction.[11]

From this theoretical approach, we would expect that the whole range of group activities, not just social life, would be influenced by the interaction pattern fostered by the job. The previously cited study by the University of Liverpool researchers, for example, notes that dockworkers who were members of semipermanent crews were rarely found among the informal leaders of the longshoremen or among the active participants in the union.[12] Moving in the other direction, Lipset concludes that because some jobs handicap workers in maintaining adequate off-the-job relations with other friends (e.g., unusual working hours as among printers, actors, and policemen), they tend to form more closely knit "fellow worker" groups, as evidenced by their record of high participation in local union activities.[13]

Similarly, George Strauss has observed an unusually high degree of membership participation in certain occupational groups involving relative isolation from fellow workers, like insurance salesmen, utility meter readers and substation operators.[14]

Such studies add to the trend toward considering the *need for social relations* as a variable worth studying in itself. It would be interesting to know, for example, whether industrial occupations in which there is high inter-worker dependence in the work process, such that almost constant interaction is required, show less social life than groups characterized by relatively independent operations.

[10] Chris Argyris, *Organization of a Bank* (New Haven: Labor and Management Center, Yale University, 1954), p. 129.

[11] Eliot D. Chapple, "Applied Anthropology in Industry," in *Anthropology Today,* A. L. Kroeber, ed. (Chicago: University of Chicago Press, 1953), pp. 819-831. Many of the observations in this section are based on the theoretical work of Chapple.

[12] University of Liverpool, *op. cit.,* p. 72.

[13] Seymour M. Lipset, "The Political Process in Trade Unions: A Theoretical Statement," in *Freedom and Control in Modern Society,* Monroe Berger, Theodore Abel, and Charles Page, eds. (New York: Van Nostrand, 1954), pp. 101-102.

[14] Personal correspondence, Professor Strauss, University of Buffalo.

The Task Group

Perhaps one of the most important aspects of small group behavior in large organizations is their relation to the work process itself. The formally designated task builds a group structure, just as do individual social needs and the organizational authority structure.

More specifically, the work process stimulates group controls of (a) work method, (b) output standards or productivity, and (c) relative compensation and prestige relationships.

(a) *Impact on Work Method.* The experience of working in close proximity on a day-to-day basis induces methods that may depart from the organization's original conception of the job, or at least "fills in" the specific details of the operation not specified in the formal work plan. Thus, employees may exchange repetitive jobs, although such trading is illegal; one worker may do two jobs while a colleague rests; or, as Whyte[15] found, they may change the sequence of the operations to reduce tensions and provide short cuts. Roy observed similar "adjustments" in relations among tool room clerks, job setters, and machinists where the objective was maximizing piece rate earnings.[16]

Some of these informal, or unplanned for, work methods may decrease worker output. For example, workers' machinations in Roy's machine shop tended to overstate make-ready time during job changes. However, other worker innovations, such as those described by Whyte, undoubtedly increase the total product. Gross found that radar teams, through communication circuits set up during off-the-job social periods, were compensating for deficiencies in the information provided by the formal organization.[17]

Similarly researchers have analyzed the initiative exhibited by a group of department store salesmen in evolving a new work pattern

[15] William F. Whyte, "The Social Structure of the Restaurant," *The American Journal of Sociology*, LIV (January 1949), pp. 306-307.

[16] Donald Roy, "Quota Restriction and Goldbricking in a Machine Shop," *The American Journal of Sociology*, LVII (March 1952), pp. 427-442.

[17] Edward Gross, "Some Functional Consequences of Primary Controls in Formal Work Organizations," *American Sociological Review*, XVIII (August 1953), pp. 370-371.

that solved a serious internal morale problem created by a new incentive system.[18]

However, the work structure can be designed so that elaborations of the informal group necessarily work in opposition to the major objectives of the organization. Recent studies of changes in the method of mining coal, conducted by the Tavistock Institute in Great Britain, illustrate such organization.[19] The change from jobs completed by small groups of miners in one shift to successive operations carried out by three shifts resulted in reduction of interaction and communication and a consequent decrease in the miners' recognition of their total responsibility for the operation.[20]

Thus the Tavistock studies suggest that the goal of the engineer in designing the technological organization is to provide the work group with a relatively autonomous task so that responsible *internal* leadership can develop. This kind of organizational structure is, in fact, the very essence of decentralization:

> A primary work organization of this type has the advantage of placing responsibility for the complete . . . task squarely on the shoulders of a single, small, face-to-face group which experiences the entire cycle of operations within the compass of its membership. For each participant the task has total significance and dynamic closure.[21]

The development of mutually convenient methods of conducting the work process can extend to the "job" of collective bargaining. We have ample evidence that union-management relationships at the work group level often depart radically from established practices and attitudes prevailing at higher levels, and may in fact contradict these other, more "formal" relationships.[22]

Aside from evolving methods which seem most convenient to

[18] Nicholas Babchuck and William Coode, "Work Incentives in a Self-Determined Group," *American Sociological Review*, XVI (October 1951), p. 686.

[19] E. Trist and K. Bamforth, "Some Social and Psychological Consequences of the Long Wall Method of Coal-Getting," *Human Relations*, IV, No. 1 (1951).

[20] The same problem can arise even though the employees are not separated into different time shifts. A study of a textile mill provides us with an example of the impact of worker-machine allocations. Cf. A. K. Rice, "Productivity and Social Organization in an Indian Weaving Shed," *Human Relations*, VI, No. 4 (1953).

[21] Trist and Bamforth, *op. cit.*, p. 6.

[22] Cf. Melville Dalton, "Unofficial Union-Management Relations," *American Sociological Review*, XV (October 1950), pp. 611-619.

work group members, the pattern of doing the job is fitted to the status system of the group. Those members with most prestige, if at all possible, receive the best jobs. Where possible, working location and equipment are similarly "assigned." And where these are not under group control, helping and trading can be adjusted to the status system. The exchange-of-favors system readily responds to the prestige hierarchy. Of course, the evaluation placed on jobs is itself a product of group interaction.

The methods evolved within the group for task completion become firmly established. Where outside forces (e.g., technological change) threaten to induce changes, the ranks close and resistance is applied. In part, of course, this may be the natural reaction of the culprit fearing punishment for rule infractions. A more reasonable explanation of the informal group's resistance to change, however, is the intimate relationship between the task group as an entity and the work methods they have evolved. A threat to one is a real threat to the other.

(b) *Impact on Output Standards.* Probably more attention has been given to this aspect of task group behavior than to any other. Starting with the work of Mathewson, and extending through the Western Electric studies, a long and distinguished line of studies indicate that work groups often formulate quite specific output standards and obtain close conformity from their members in *maintaining* these standards. Productivity itself is increasingly conceived as a group phenomenon.

Several reasons have been advanced as to why output control occupies a place of such importance in the life of the group. Work standards are one of the most important aspects of the job, which can in some fashion be influenced by worker action. The energy expenditure required by the job is largely determined by the number of units required, rather than by the nature of the job itself. Presumably without group control management would be able to utilize individual differences, and competition for promotion and greater earnings, to obtain higher and higher standards. This would penalize particularly the slower worker and the older employee. It might, however, penalize all workers by cutting piece rates, where such exist, and/or reducing the number of employees required by the operation. "Run away" output might have internal ramifications.

We have observed situations where group controls were weak, and younger, low-prestige employees exceeded the production and earnings records of their "betters." The results were calamitous for the status hierarchy of the department and ultimately for the effectiveness of the formal organization.

Output control is a basic objective of group action as well as an essential element in maintaining group stability. Not only the relationship of the members to one another, but the durability of the worker relationship to his job depends on the efficacy of this process. Again we need to note that the resultant is not always unfavorable to management. We have many instances on record where the group has sanctioned increasingly high productivity,[23] rejected fellow workers who could not maintain high output, and resisted threats to existing high quality standards.

Evidently a great deal of the interest in "informal group relations" is the result of this presumed relationship between output standards evolving within the group and actual worker productivity. Wilensky in an earlier chapter reviews some of the efforts to find the magic formula to convert group norms from "low" to "high."

Some of the earliest research on productivity was based on the assumption that internal harmony in the work group would produce higher performance records. Increasingly researchers have become disillusioned with the relationship between social satisfaction and worker effort. Perhaps one of the most telling blows to the impetus to devote substantial energies to building work groups that are "sociometrically sound" is the provocative study by Goode and Fowler in a low morale plant. They found "the informal relationships which developed were such as to maintain pressures toward high production in the face of considerable *animosity* toward the owners and *among the workers themselves*."[24] While their findings are severely limited by the somewhat unique environment they chose, it has become recognized that the relationship between friendship and output is a complex one.

[23] Cf. George Strauss, "Group Dynamics and Intergroup Relations," in William F. Whyte and others, *Money and Motivation* (New York: Harper, 1955), pp. 90-96.

[24] William Goode and Irving Fowler, "Incentive Factors in a Low Morale Plant," *American Sociological Review,* XIV (October 1949), p. 624; italics added by author.

More recently, Seashore finds in a study in a large "heavy equipment manufacturing company" that highly "cohesive" work groups are more likely to have output records that diverge *in either direction* from plant averages.[25] By implication, then, tightly knit work groups are almost as likely to have notably *poor* production records as outstandingly *good* ones.

The present author is inclined to believe that these inconsistencies in research results are due to an overemphasis on output as a part of informal group equilibrium. Control over output is also a major weapon in the arsenal of the group engaging in conflict with management, other work groups, and even the local union. We need to know more about the *total situation* facing a given work group, including these external factors, before predicting its work performance.

The evolution of the method of *group decision* for gaining acceptance for changes in production methods and output standards is recognition of the potency of group standards. The theory presumes that leadership methods that involve the entire work group in the change process have two major advantages:

1. They can eliminate the major barrier of existing group standards which militate against any change, per se.
2. More positively, they commit the individual to new efforts in the context of his group membership. In a sense, the individual "promises" his fellows to accomplish some change in his behavior. Valuing the opinions of his associates, he feels bound to maintain his agreement.

Ideally the "decision" itself becomes the new standard or norm of conduct for the task group. Similarly efforts to develop plant-wide incentive systems are premised on the assumption that output and effort are dependent on the relation of the work group to the total social system of the plant.[26]

(c) *Impact on Relative Compensation and Prestige Relationships.* The fact that jobs take on a significant social meaning can be seen in the importance attached to wage differentials within the group itself. For example, we have many instances on record when man-

[25] Stanley Seashore, *Group Cohesiveness in the Industrial Work Group* (Ann Arbor: Institute for Social Research, University of Michigan, 1954), p. 98.

[26] Cf. William F. Whyte and others, *Money and Motivation, op. cit.*, p. 225.

agement assigned an equal value to each job and the group found significant distinguishing characteristics. Jobs ranked by employees as *more important or desirable* are expected to have higher earnings than jobs ranked below. The established hierarchy is reinforced over time by the gradual perfection of the correlation between esteem accorded particular workers and prestige accorded to their jobs. The "more important" workers have moved to the "more important" jobs. (The importance attached to the job is not only a function of the earning capacity but also the quality of the surroundings, equipment, the tempo of the work required, etc.) Problems occur only when changes are introduced which violate the established hierarchy.

A persistent problem has been that jobs which the group evaluates as relatively undesirable may need to be compensated at a higher rate than the "desirable" jobs, in order to attract adequate personnel. However, this differential may be contrary to the status system of the work group. Similarly, jobs evaluated (by the group) as desirable may lack characteristics which would bring them a high rating under the organization's formal ranking plan. These contradictions between the group and the organization's ranking system become more important during periods of relative labor shortage, when new recruits are difficult to obtain and when the group undergoes aging.

While these several concepts of the "informal group" are not identical, and in some cases not even complementary in their basic dimensions, they do have one common feature. All stress equilibrium, the development of a system of interpersonal relations which stabilizes the work situation (among subordinates and between superior and subordinates), an interconnected series of friendship linkages, work flow relationships, output levels, and status-income relations. The objectives are the maintenance of individual and group stability by insuring a predictability of day-to-day events and effecting a *modus vivendi* as between individual on-the-job needs and the requirements of the formal organization.

As such, the *informal group* in any and all of its meanings is serving well-recognized and accepted human needs. Its existence and continued preservation are hardly matters for surprise. The building up of routines, of established methods of accomplishing tasks, of predictable social relationships, of group roles—these are all elements of structuring which social scientists have found typical of the human group. In fact, the elements define the group.

Particularly through the setting and maintenance of group standards, informal groups have protected their memberships from possible indiscretions that might reflect adversely on them all; also they have provided support for the individual, by acting as a buffer to outside organizations and by sustaining him through the provision of *known and acceptable* routines of behaving within the face-to-face work group.

Thus the informal group, as perceived in such studies, *reacts to* the initiations of other organizations, particularly management. Being defined in equilibrium terms, the reaction is always an attempt to *regain* the previous undisturbed state—to protect work methods, social relationships, and output levels incorporated in the norms of the group.

Concerted Interest as the Focus

Workers also band together into *interest groups.* These are formed not only to protect their members but also to exploit *opportunities* to improve their relative position. Improvements can take the form of "looser standards," a preferred seniority position, more overtime, more sympathetic supervision, correction of "inequities," better equipment, and countless other less tangible goals that make the job a better one and that often serve to substitute for the more traditional kinds of promotions and mobility.

Distribution of these benefits may be much influenced by pressures of united and determined informal groups. What management feels is "equitable," just as what the union determines is in the "members' interest," is determined to a large extent by attitudes expressed by those individuals who can support their demands by group reinforcements. Those work groups which for one reason or another are unable to exercise similar power in the market place of the plant are penalized.

This is not the traditional concept of the informal group seeking conformity with established norms of conduct. These are much more "free enterprise" units, interacting in a struggle for maximization of utility. All are not equally aggressive in the struggle for self-improvement or equally well equipped with the wherewithal to do battle via the grievance procedure and the more direct pressure tactics on union and management. Some lack the spirit of combat, others the means, while only a restricted few are endowed with the characteristics associated with sustained "activity" and progress toward the goals they seek.

Much of what we say implies a degree of dual or even treble *disloyalty*. Other groups, management, the union, and fellow workers, are perceived as either barriers or sources of assistance. From the point of view of the interest group, it is not high identification or loyalty that counts, but rather the right tactics in using or ignoring these other aggregations.

Thus, management is neither "good" nor "bad," liked or disliked as such. In fact, this approach suggests that it may not always be fruitful to think in pro-management and pro-union terms. It may well be that a group which is satisfied with *itself*, with its ability to protect and improve its own interests, is more favorable to *both* union and management.[27]

The results for the larger plant may not be a system tending toward equilibrium at all. We might expect that certain combinations of pressure groups actually involve the organization in increasing instability—a trend toward disequilibrium. We have observed plants where the interaction of these groups involves increasingly greater discontent, turmoil, and nonadaptive behavior. That is, their behavior tends to reinforce the very problems it was designed to solve.

Similarly, the internal structure of these groups is much more responsive to changes in its external environment than is often implied in the concept of the informal work group as a relatively durable, impervious entity. Literally overnight, technical changes introduced by management can convert a cohesive task force into a disunited, apathetic "rabble," squabbling over internal differences. Similarly, we have observed a group of weakly-united employees become a force of some magnitude in the social system of the plant within a brief period, with no changes in personnel.

The existence of these *interest group* types suggests that greater

[27] These areas will be further elaborated in the author's forthcoming study, *Technology and Work Group Behavior* (Ann Arbor: Bureau of Industrial Relations, University of Michigan, 1956).

attention should be given to matching supervisory "types" with group "types." We have tended to think of effective supervision as being the product of a relationship between a good leader and his group, on the assumption that the group of subordinates was a constant. In fact, variations in the effectiveness of supervision may be as much due to inherent differences in the group itself as to the leadership practices exhibited by the supervisor.

THE INTERNAL DYNAMICS OF THE WORK GROUP

We have concentrated primarily on the relationship of the small group to the larger organization, the functions served, the "compatibilities" and "incompatibilities." Therefore, we have failed to explore much of the research that stresses the intriguing inner processes of these groups, as semiautonomous organizations. This means neglecting the processes of self-selection and exclusion developed in the work of Moreno and his colleagues in the field of sociometry. We have also omitted the prolific findings of the "group dynamics school" with its emphasis on leadership patterns and role differentiation, factors contributing to cohesiveness, and the impact of the group itself on membership perceptions and attitudes. Bales and his associates at Harvard have probed deeply into the "ebb and flow" of the problem-solving process within the group. The sequential member roles have been analyzed effectively.

For our purposes it would seem appropriate at least to make specific reference to the work of George Homans. His work places substantial emphasis on the relationship of the internal life of the group to the outside environment (primarily the attitudes, organizational structure, and work method induced by management).[28] "Elaborations" of behavior and sentiment induced in the small group in turn modify the larger organization. While we believe an overemphasis on the concept of *equilibrium* may be misleading, Homans' theorizing does provide a framework within which to relate the small group to the larger organization of which it is a part.

CONCLUSION

Clusterings of workers-on-the-job all have these characteristics: They stem from the uniqueness of individual personality, which

[28] George Homans, *The Human Group* (New York: Harcourt Brace, 1950).

refuses to combine into larger "wholes" without changing those entities. The sum of a group of individuals is something more than the total of the constituents; it is a new organization, because most of the members (there are significant exceptions as we have noted) obtain satisfaction in gaining acceptance as a part of the group, and the group itself wields an influence over its members. Put in another way, there are pressures toward *conformity* within the group. These pressures result in the establishment of accepted ways of living together. The way of life of the group includes a complex system of customs and rules, vested interests, and interaction patterns which govern the relationship of members of the group to one another and to the larger environment of which it is a part.

This observance of group-sanctioned behavior and attitudes "fills out" the rationally conceived organization. What is on paper an organization becomes a "living, breathing" social organism, with all the intricacies, emotions, and contradictions we associate with human relations. While no organization would long persist which did not provide its members with this opportunity for spontaneous "human relations," a major problem of the larger organization becomes one of successfully incorporating the small group.

· X ·

STUDYING AND CREATING CHANGE: A MEANS TO UNDERSTANDING SOCIAL ORGANIZATION

BY FLOYD C. MANN*
University of Michigan

Social organizations are functioning entities with interdependent structures and processes. They are not fixed, static structures, but rather continuously moving patterns of relationships in a much larger field of social activity. To understand what their essential elements and dimensions are, what it is that gives an organization its unity, it is necessary to study and create social change within organizational settings.

Relatively little is known about organizational change. Social scientists stress the study of the dynamic in social systems, but few[1] accept the risks involved to gain the knowledge and skills needed to create and measure changes in functioning organizations. This is not surprising, for research within large-scale organizations is at such an early stage that the social scientist knows little about how (1) to

* Drs. Rensis Likert, Daniel Katz, Robert Kahn, and Norman R. F. Maier have made especially helpful suggestions concerning the organization and presentation of this material. They can, of course, in no way be held responsible for the shortcomings which remain.

[1] For an account of a conspicuous exception to this, see N. C. Mare and E. Reimer, "The Experimental Manipulation of a Major Organizational Variable," in *Journal of Abnormal and Social Psychology* (1956).

gain access to these research sites, (2) to initiate and sustain organizational change, and (3) to measure such changes. We have only begun the systematic codification of the working knowledge and skills necessary for the researcher to get into, and maintain himself within, the social science laboratories of functioning organizations.[2] Systematic, quantitative measurement of change processes in complex organizational settings is in its infancy. Longitudinal studies are rare—social scientists seldom attempt to obtain more than a single "before" and "after" measurement and are often content to try and decipher findings from *ex post facto* study designs. The actual steps and skills necessary to initiate and sustain changes within an organization are not only relatively unknown, but there is even some suspicion that knowledge of social action and an ability to engineer change are not appropriate for the social scientist.

While social scientists are not spending any sizable proportion of their time in learning how to change interpersonal and intergroup relations in functioning organizations, a wide variety of practitioners are. These include at the one extreme the consultants or the "operators" who take over organizations which are failing and rebuild them, and at the other extreme, the "human relations" trainers. Most of these men know very little theoretically about processes of organizational, attitudinal, and behavioral change, but they do know a great deal intuitively about the problems of changing people in an organization. This is especially true of the training men.

This suggests that there should and can be a closer working relationship between those concerned with actually *changing* organizational structure and processes and those researchers concerned with *understanding* organizational change. Social scientists have not begun to take advantage of their opportunities for learning about organizations from those in the "practicing professions"—those who are *doing*.[3] Observations and systematic measurements around the practitioner's efforts to alter systems of relationships in organizations can provide the researcher with valuable insights into the dynamics of organization. Gaps in knowledge become excruciatingly apparent; new sources of data and problems for research emerge.

[2] F. Mann and R. Lippitt, eds., "Social Relations Skills in Field Research," *Journal of Social Issues*, VIII, No. 3 (1952).

[3] Donald Young, "Sociology and the Practicing Professions," *American Sociological Review*, XX (December 1955), pp. 641-648.

In turn, social scientists can contribute to practitioners by helping them assess what effect their actions as change agents have. Most practitioners—and especially those trainers who are concerned with changing the human relations skills of supervisors—have very little systematic, and no quantitative, evidence on the success of their efforts to create changes in individuals or organizations. It seems clear that there is a broad basis for cooperation here. Systematic studies of the work of those attempting to change the way things are done in an organization may contribute to our understanding of social organizations. And developments in measurement and the procedures used by researchers to understand organizations better may contribute to the working knowledge of trainers and others in the "practicing professions."

In this chapter we will focus on the description and evaluation of several different types of procedures designed to change interpersonal and intergroup relations in complex organizations. We will first look at two human relations training programs whose effects have been systematically and quantitatively studied. Then we will describe briefly the development and evaluation of a change procedure with which we are experimenting to increase the understanding, acceptance, and utilization of survey research findings. At the close of the chapter these two specific types of procedures for creating change in organizational settings are contrasted as a first step in identifying facets of change processes which merit greater experimentation and in providing insights into the structure and functioning of organizations.

CHANGING INTERPERSONAL RELATIONS THROUGH TRAINING SUPERVISORS

Recurrent opportunities for social scientists to study a change process within an organizational setting are provided by human relations training programs for supervisors. As change procedures, these programs are formal, rational, purposeful efforts to alter institutional behavior. In contrast to the day-to-day attempts of management to bring about change, they are bounded in time and organizational space, and are thus easily studied intensively.

Because of the several historical developments described in Chapters I, II, and XIII, management by the late forties began to be convinced that training might be useful for their supervisors, and there has since been a wholesale adoption of human relations training programs. While there was and still is a remarkable range in the content, methods, and settings of these programs, nearly all of them have centered around improving supervisory skills in dealing with people—either as individuals or in face-to-face groups. They are frequently directed at teaching the supervisor how to work with an employee as an individual, occasionally at working with employees as members of a small group, but only rarely at understanding and working within the complex social system of the large corporation or factory. Another way of saying this is that the courses have drawn heavily from psychology, to a lesser extent from social psychology, and usually not at all from sociology.

There are no commonly agreed-upon ways by which these programs can be described. The following headings are, however, useful: objectives, content, methods, setting, training leader, and training unit. For example, the objectives of these programs are usually very general and quite ambitious: "to assist supervisors in developing the skills, knowledge, and attitudes needed to carry out their supervisory responsibilities," or "to improve morale, increase production, and reduce turnover." Their contents usually include human nature, personality, motivation, attitudes, and leadership, and other information about relevant psychological principles and research findings may also be included. More often than not the methods of training are some variant of the "lecture-discussion method." The settings are frequently in a classroom away from the job. The trainers are generally staff men whom the trainee did not know before the training; the trainees, first-line supervisors or foremen meeting with other supervisors from other parts of the organization.

Few systematic, quantitative studies have been made to investigate the effectiveness of these programs.[4] This is not to say that there has been no interest in evaluation. Any review of the literature will indicate many such attempts and many testimonials about

[4] A nonquantitative, but extraordinarily thorough and insightful study of foreman training was made by A. Zalenznik, *Foreman Training in a Growing Enterprise* (Boston: Graduate School of Business Administration, Harvard University, 1951).

the relative advantages of different procedures of training. Mahler and Monroe[5] reported a number of "evaluative studies" after reviewing the literature and conducting a survey of 150 companies known to have training programs. While these studies almost without fail acclaim the many benefits of such training, few of them meet more than a fraction of the requirements necessary for a rigorous test of the basic underlying assumptions.

What are these assumptions? In general, they are that training supervisors in human relations will result in changes in the supervisors' attitudes and philosophy, that these changes will be reflected in their behavior toward employees on the job, that this changed behavior will be seen by the employees, and that they will in turn become more satisfied with their work situation, then more highly motivated, and, ultimately, more productive workers.

While there is a good deal of evidence that human relations training programs do meet part of these assumptions—e.g., they do appear to change the verbal veneer of supervisors—there are few scientifically rigorous, quantitative studies which have demonstrated that these changes in what supervisors *know* affect their attitudes and behavior as seen or experienced by their subordinates. Few studies show that human relations training of supervisors is related to changes in the attitudes or productivity of employees under those supervisors.

It is not possible to make a complete review of these studies here. A review of the findings from several recent, major evaluative studies will, however, provide a good deal of evidence concerning the effectiveness of certain types of training programs. The findings will certainly emphasize the need for more systematic, quantitative research to assess the most effective combinations of content, methods, settings, training units, and trainers.

The Canter-Tyler Studies

In 1949, Canter[6] developed a human relations training course for first-line supervisors in the home offices of a large insurance com-

[5] W. R. Mahler and W. H. Monroe, *How Industry Determines the Need for and Effectiveness of Training*, Personnel Research Section Report 929 (Washington: Department of the Army, 1952).

[6] R. R. Canter, "A Human Relations Training Program," *Journal of Applied Psychology*, XXXV (February 1951), pp. 38-45.

pany. The three objectives of the course were "(1) to establish facts and principles concerning psychological aspects of behavior and group functioning to enable supervisors to become more competent in their knowledge and understanding of human behavior; (2) to increase supervisors' capacities for observing human behavior; and (3) to present personality adjustment concepts to aid in integration of achievements made in the first two objectives." This training was designed to provide a foundation of information on which to build later through additional practice and "technique" training. Specific content was primarily psychological: human nature, personality, motivation, attitudes, leadership, and group structure. Method was lecture-discussion. The training occurred in the conference rooms of the company; Canter himself was the trainer. The trainees were eighteen supervisors whose superiors had participated in a preliminary run for executives. The course was presented in ten two-hour weekly sessions.

To determine the influence of this training, Canter employed a battery of paper-and-pencil questionnaires and tests which were given before and after training to two groups of supervisors: an experimental group of eighteen from one department who received the training, and a control group of eighteen from two other departments who did not receive training. The two groups were similar in type of work performed, age (about thirty), education (thirteen years), and proportion of men and women. While the control group had more years of service with the company (7.5 and 4.6, respectively) and higher mean scores on a mental alertness test, the statistical technique used in the final analysis did not require prematched individuals or groups.

Six tests, yielding a total of twelve separate scores, were used. (1) General Psychological Facts and Principles; (2) "How Supervise"; (3) General Logical Reasoning; (4) Social Judgment Test; (5) Supervisory Questionnaire; and (6) Test for Ability to Estimate Group Opinion. The major findings were that the trained supervisors obtained mean scores on all tests better than would have been predicted on the basis of the performance of the untrained group alone. For five out of the twelve measures, the differences were statistically significant at the 5 per cent level; for two other measures, differences were significant at the 10 per cent level. Other important conclusions were that trained supervisors became more similar in abilities measured by the tests and more accurate in estimating the opinions of employees in their departments, but not their sections. It was also found that those holding highest scores initially gained the most on all measures except the Test of Ability to Estimate Group Opinion, where the opposite result was obtained.

While Canter assumed in his design that cognitive training—i.e., an ability to understand human relations concepts and principles—would have to precede any behavioral training in supervisory skills, practices, and attitudes, Tyler[7] designed a companion study to measure any changes in employee morale which might be attributed to this training. Her morale surveys indicated improvement in employee morale scores for *both* the experimental and control departments. Morale improved by an average of 11 points per section (range 2-25 points) in five of seven sections in the experimental group, and decreased slightly in two others. "In the control groups, morale increased in eight of the nine sections by an average of 14 points (range 5-32 points). The decrease in the other section was seven points. The only category which showed a somewhat consistent change among sections was 'supervision' on which scores for over half of the sections decreased." After warning the reader of the possible effect of the before-test experience, she notes: "Undoubtedly, the difference in change in morale between the control and the experimental groups is not large enough to be significant" (page 47). Canter, however, points out that in Tyler's study "morale was quite high initially, which might account for the lack of any improvement in the experimental department over the control."

The strength of the Canter-Tyler studies is that they used both *before* and *after* measures for experimental and control groups. Canter's use of multiple criteria against which to evaluate the various sub-goals of the training program is also noteworthy. The use of Tyler's perceptual and employee morale measures in conjunction with Canter's attitudinal and cognitive measures permits an evaluation of the course's effectiveness at two levels: the supervisor's intent, and his on-the-job performance. The findings from this combination of studies make it obvious that classroom learning does

[7] B. B. Tyler, "A Study of Factors Contributing to Employee Morale" (Master's thesis, Ohio State University, 1949).

not guarantee the translation of such learning into job performance. It should be remembered, however, that Canter did not set out to change supervisors' skills and practices, but only their understanding of human relations concepts and ideas.

Fleishman-Harris Studies

Working with the education and training staff of a large company manufacturing trucks and farm machinery, Fleishman[8] developed a study design and a battery of research instruments for measuring the continuing effectiveness of leadership training. The general objectives of this training[9] were to change understanding, attitudes, habits, and skills of foremen by giving them solid foundation in four basic areas of industrial knowledge. These areas were personal development, human relations, economics, and company operations. The method was primarily lecture-discussion. The training staff included full-time instructors, former supervisors, and part-time university faculty. The training was given to foremen who were taken from a wide variety of operations and plants and sent to a central school in Chicago for two weeks of eight-hours-a-day intensive development.

To determine the effects of this course on foremen from one motor-truck plant who had taken this training, Fleishman employed an *ex post facto* design with four groups of about thirty each. One group had not received the training; the other three had, 2-10, 11-19, and 20-29 months earlier. The groups were alike on a number of background characteristics: age (early forties), education (eleven years), length of service (sixteen years), supervisory experience (seven years), size of work group (about twenty-eight), and supervisory experience with present work group (six years). Seven paper-and-pencil questionnaires were used to obtain opinion, expectation, and perceptual data about leadership practices from the trainees, their superiors, and their subordinates. This battery gave Fleishman an opportunity to investigate the differences between supervisory beliefs as reported by the foreman himself and supervisory practices as reported by his employees, and to explore the interaction of train-

[8] Edwin A. Fleishman, "Leadership Climate, Human Relations Training, and Supervisory Behavior," *Personnel Psychology*, VI (Summer 1953), pp. 205-222.

[9] Charles L. Walker, Jr., "Education and Training at International Harvester," *Harvard Business Review*, XXVII (September 1949), pp. 542-558.

ing effects with the supervisor's "leadership climate." Each questionnaire contained two independent leadership dimensions which had been identified by factor analysis: "consideration"—the extent to which the supervisor was considerate of the feelings of employees; and "initiating structure"—the extent to which the supervisor defined or facilitated group interactions toward goal attainment.

The results obtained by giving attitude questionnaires to foremen on the first and last days of their training in Chicago provide evidence of how the topics stressed in this leadership training affected these two dimensions. The results obtained from these before and after measures showed a significant increase in "consideration" (.05 level) and an even more marked decrease in "initiating structure" (.01 level). The on-the-job effects of the training, however, appeared to be "minimal." "The training did not produce any kind of permanent change in either the attitudes or behavior of the trained foremen." The employees under the most recently trained foremen actually saw them as *less* considerate than the employees under the untrained foremen saw their superiors. This statistically significant finding was supported by other trends toward more structuring and less consideration by those foremen who had the training. Thus, while the human relations approach was stressed in the course and understood at least well enough to be regisered as an opinion change on a paper-and-pencil questionnaire, it was not evident in what trained foremen said they did, or what their employees saw them doing in the actual work situation.

The most important variable found to affect leadership was the climate within which the foreman worked. In fact, the kind of superior under whom the foreman operated seemed "more related to the attitudes and behavior of the foremen in the plant than did the fact that they had or had not received the leadership training."

These results, showing that the training was not meeting its objective of making foremen more human-relations oriented in the plant, left two alternatives open: redesign the course, or initiate an intensive criterion study relating supervisory behavior to group effectiveness. The latter alternative was chosen, and Harris[10] designed a study in the same plant to investigate (1) the relationship

[10] E. F. Harris, "Measuring Industrial Leadership and Its Implications for Training Supervisors" (Doctoral thesis, Ohio State University, 1952).

between these two dimensions of leadership behavior and various measures of work efficiency, and (2) the effects of a training course planned as a brief refresher for the central school training in Chicago. It is the findings from this second objective in which we are primarily interested here.

The course, lasting one week, was given at a small nearby college. The effects were evaluated by field experimental design with before and after measures for experimental and control groups. Two groups of thirty-one foremen were established through matching on a number of variables, including length of time since attending the central school (almost three years), scores on before measures (including leadership climate), and other personal factors. One group was given the training. Questionnaires, similar to Fleishman's, were used to obtain information from employees and foremen about the foremen's attitudes and behavior.

Harris used several different methods of analyzing his findings. His most rigorous method indicated there were no statistically significant differences in the foremen's own leadership attitudes or the workers' descriptions of their foremen's behavior—before and after this additional refresher course. The only significant difference he found was a decrease in the degree to which the foremen in the *control* group showed structuring in their leadership behavior as described by their employees. Building on Fleishman's gradual decreases in structuring and increases in consideration the longer the foreman is back on the job, Harris suggests this finding might be interpreted to mean that the refresher course may have "tended to retard a general decrease in structuring."

Harris and Fleishman[11] in analyzing the data from both of their studies in the same plant have uncovered one finding which tends to qualify the general, completely negative conclusion of their findings regarding the effectiveness of this training. This finding concerns the stability of leadership patterns of individual foremen who did not have the training in contrast to those foremen who had the training. They find there is *less* stability in the pre-post measures for the foremen who had the training than for those foremen who did not have training. This suggests that the courses had markedly

[11] E. F. Harris and E. A. Fleishman, "Human Relations Training and the Stability of Leadership Patterns," *Journal of Applied Psychology*, XXXIX (February 1955), pp. 20-25.

different effects on different foremen, and that "large individual shifts in scores occur in both directions." They conclude that their research findings show no significant changes in *group* means among trained foremen and that future research should be directed toward investigating personal and situational variables which interact with the effects of training.

At best, these two studies suggest that this type of training has little or no general effect on the behavior of foremen in the plant. At worst, they suggest that the unanticipated consequences of separating foremen from their work groups and making them keenly aware of their role in management more than offset the anticipated consequences of making the foremen more considerate of employees as human beings. Fleishman's finding that *leadership climate* appeared to be a better predictor than *training* of foremen's plant attitudes and behavior underscores the importance of considering the constellation of expectation patterns in which the trainee is embedded. Training which does not take the trainee's regular social environment into account will probably have little chance of modifying behavior. It may very well be that human relations training—as a procedure for initiating social change—is most successful when it is designed to *remold the whole system of role relationships of the supervisor.*[12]

The findings from these four studies suggest that trainers, researchers, and others interested in social change need to rethink what forces are necessary to create and sustain changes in the orientation and behaviors of people in complex systems of relationships. There is a good deal of evidence that management and trainees are enthusiastic about these training courses in general. Management's enthusiasm may be an index of whether the training will continue, but it does not indicate whether training is achieving changes in behavior. And while trainee satisfaction and acceptance may be important as an antecedent to learning, these factors do not indicate whether the training will produce attitudinal and, more significantly, on-the-job behavioral changes.

It should be stressed that the criterion which has been used here

[12] For a full account of these two studies combined, see E. A. Fleishman, E. F. Harris, and H. E. Buntt, *Leadership and Supervision in Industry* (Columbus: Personnel Research Board, Ohio State University, 1955).

for measuring the effects of human relations training is not easily met. There is ample quantitative evidence in the preceding studies that supervisors' information about, and verbal understanding of, human relations principles can be increased. There is much less evidence that these courses have an effect on the trainee's on-the-job behavior as seen by those working under him. And the hard fact remains that there are no quantitative studies which indicate that these courses in leadership affect workers' job satisfactions or motivations.

FEEDBACK: CHANGING PATTERNS OF RELATIONSHIPS BETWEEN SUPERIORS AND SUBORDINATES BY USING SURVEY FINDINGS

Long-range interest in the actual varying of significant variables in organizations has necessitated that members of the Human Relations Program of the Institute for Social Research, University of Michigan, not only study existing programs for training and changing people in organizations, but that we *develop* new techniques for changing relationships, and that we learn how to *measure* the effects of such changes within organizations. As a result, we have invested a good deal of professional effort in exploring the effectiveness of different procedures for changing attitudes, perceptions, and relationships among individuals in complex hierarchies without changing the personnel of the units. The latter is an important qualification, for we have found that the changes in subordinates' perceptions and attitudes which follow a change in supervisory personnel are frequently of a much larger order than those generated by training or other procedures for changing the attitudes or behavior of incumbents.

Exploratory and Developmental Phase

One procedure which we developed and subsequently found to be effective in changing perceptions and relationships within organizations has been called "feedback." This change process evolved over a period of years as we[13] tried to learn how to report findings

[13] A number of people contributed to the design of this feedback process during its developmental phase. They included Sylvester Leahy, Blair Swartz, Robert Schwab, and John Sparling from the Detroit Edison Company, and Rensis Likert, Daniel Katz, Everett Riemer, Frances Fielder, and Theodore Hariton from the Survey Research Center.

from human relations research into organizations so that they would be understood and used in day-to-day operations. Work began on this process in 1948 following a company-wide study of employee and management attitudes and opinions. Over a period of two years, three different sets of data were fed back: (1) information on the attitudes and perceptions of 8000 nonsupervisory employees toward their work, promotion opportunities, supervision, fellow employees, etc.; (2) first- and second-line supervisor's feelings about the various aspects of their jobs and supervisory beliefs; and (3) information from intermediate and top levels of management about their supervisory philosophies, roles in policy formation, problems of organizational integration, etc. We had several aims in this exploratory phase: (1) to develop through first-hand experience an understanding of the problems of producing change; (2) to improve relationships; (3) to identify factors which affected the extent of the change; and (4) to develop working hypotheses for later, more directed research.

The process which finally appeared to maximize the acceptance and utilization of survey and research findings can be described structurally as an interlocking chain of conferences. It began with a report of the major findings of the survey to the president and his senior officers, and then progressed slowly down through the hierarchical levels along functional lines to where supervisors and their employees were discussing the data. These meetings were structured in terms of organizational "families"[14] or units—each superior and his immediate subordinates considering the survey data together. The data presented to each group were those pertaining to their own group or for those subunits for which members of the organizational unit were responsible.

Members of each group were asked to help interpret the data and then decide what further analyses of the data should be made to aid them in formulating plans for constructive administrative actions. They also planned the introduction of the findings to the next level. The meetings were typically led by the line officer responsible for the coordination of the subunits at a particular level. Usually, a

[14] F. Mann and J. Dent, "The Supervisor: Member of Two Organizational Families," *Harvard Business Review*, XXXII (November-December 1954), pp. 103-112.

member of the Survey Research Center and the company's personnel staff assisted the line officer in preparing for these meetings, but attended the meetings only as resource people who could be called upon for information about the feasibility of additional analyses.

These meetings took place in the office of the line supervisor whose organizational unit was meeting, or in the department's own small conference room. All of the survey findings relative to each group were given to the leader and the members of his organizational unit; they decided what to consider first, how fast to work through each topic, and when they had gone as far as they could and needed to involve the next echelon in the process.

This feedback change procedure was developed in an organization where a great amount of effort had already been invested in the training of management and supervisors. During the war the company had participated in the various J-programs sponsored by the War Manpower Commission, and more important, during the several years we were experimentally developing the feedback process, Dr. Norman R. F. Maier was working with all levels of management to improve their understanding of human relations and supervision.[15] The supervisors with whom we were working to increase their understanding of their own organizational units therefore had a great deal of training in the application of psychological principles to management.

Our observations of the feedback procedure as it developed suggested that it was a powerful process for creating and supporting changes within an organization.[16] However, there was no quantitative proof of this, for our work up to this point had been exploratory and developmental.

A Field Experiment in Accounting Departments

In 1950, when eight accounting departments in this same company asked for a second attitude and opinion survey of their seventy-eight supervisors and eight hundred employees, we[17] had

[15] For a thorough description of this training, see N. R. F. Maier, *Principles of Human Relations* (New York: Wiley, 1952).

[16] F. Mann and R. Likert, "The Need for Research on Communicating Research Results," *Human Organization,* XI (Winter 1952), pp. 15-19.

[17] F. Mann and H. Baumgartel, *Survey Feedback Experiment: An Evaluation of a Program for the Utilization of Survey Findings,* monograph in preparation, Survey Research Center, University of Michigan.

an opportunity to initiate the steps necessary to measure the effects of this organizational change process. The questionnaires used in this resurvey were similar to those used in 1948 and provided the basis for a new cycle of feedback conferences. The general plan for the handling of these new resurvey data was to let everyone in the departments—employees and department heads—see the over-all findings for eight accounting departments combined as soon as they were available, and then to work intensively on their use in *some* departments, but not in others until there had been a third survey.

While our objective was to test the effectiveness of the basic pattern of feedback developed during the preceding two years, we encouraged department heads and their supervisors to develop their own variations for reporting data to their units and maximizing their use in the solution of problems. After the all-department meetings had been concluded, the chief executive of the accounting departments held a meeting with each department head in the experimental group. At this meeting, the findings for the department head's unit were thoroughly reviewed. The findings included comparisons of (1) changes in employee attitudes from 1948 to 1950, (2) attitudes in that department with those in all other departments combined, and (3) employees' perceptions of supervisory behavior with supervisory statements about their behavior. Department heads were encouraged to go ahead with feedback meetings as soon as they felt ready, tentative next steps were discussed, and assistance from the researchers and the company personnel staffs was assured. Four departments launched feedback activities which were similar to each other in purpose but somewhat different in method. The programs varied in duration (13-33 weeks), in intensity (9-65 meetings), and in the extent to which nonsupervisory employees were involved in the process. During the eighteen months that these differences were unfolding, nothing was done in two of the remaining four departments after the first all-departments meetings. This was done so they might be available as "controls." Changes in key personnel eliminated the remaining two departments from any experimental design.

A third survey of attitudes was conducted in these departments in 1952 after the natural variations in the feedback programs had run their courses. In 1950 and 1952 surveys were then used as "before" and "after" measurements, the four departmental programs as "experimental variations," with the two inactive departments as "controls."

Our findings indicate that more significant positive changes occurred in employee attitudes and perceptions in the four experimental departments than in the two control departments. This was based on two measures of change: (1) a comparison of answers to sixty-one identical questions which were asked in 1950 and 1952, and (2) of a comparison of answers to seventeen "perceived change" questions in which employees had an opportunity to indicate what types of changes had occurred since the 1950 survey. In the experimental group, a fourth of the sixty-one items showed relative mean positive changes, significant at the .05 level or better; the change for another 57 per cent of the items was also positive in direction, but not statistically significant. Major positive changes occurred in the experimental groups in how employees felt about (1) the kind of work they do (job interest, importance, and level of responsibility); (2) their supervisor (his ability to handle people, give recognition, direct their work, and represent them in handling complaints); (3) their progress in the company; and (4) their group's ability to get the job done. The seventeen perceived-change items were designed specifically to measure changes in the areas where we expected the greatest shift in perceptions. Fifteen of these showed that a significantly higher proportion of employees in the experimental than in the control departments felt that change had occurred. More employees in the experimental departments saw changes in (1) how well the supervisors in their department got along together; (2) how often their supervisors held meetings; (3) how effective these meetings were; (4) how much their supervisor understood the way employees looked at and felt about things, etc. These indicate the extent to which the feedback's effectiveness lay in increasing understanding and communication as well as changing supervisory behavior.

Comparisons of the changes among the four experimental departments showed that the three departments which had the two feedback sessions with their employees all showed positive change relative to the control departments. The change which occurred in the fourth was directionally positive, but it was not significantly different from the control departments. In general, the greatest change occurred where the survey results were discussed in both the departmental organizational units *and* the first-line organizational units. The greater the involvement of all members of the organization through their organizational families—the department heads, the first-line supervisors, *and* the employees—the greater the change.

Implications of These Findings

The basic elements of this feedback process described above are not new. They involve (1) the orderly collection of information about the functioning of a system, and (2) the reporting of this information into the system for (3) its use in making further adjustments.

Work by Hall[18] and others who have had considerable practical experience with the use of information about a system for creating change show a similarity in both action steps and basic approach. This suggests there are certain psychological and sociological facts which must be taken into consideration in attempting to change the attitudes and behavior of an *individual* or a *group of individuals* in an *organizational setting.*

1. Attitudes and behavior of an individual are functions of both basic personality and social role. *Change processes need to be concerned with altering both the forces within* an individual and the forces in the *organizational situation* surrounding the individual.

2. Organizations, as systems of hierarchically ordered, interlocking roles with rights and privileges, reciprocal expectations, and shared frames of reference, contain tremendous forces for stability or change in the behavior of individuals or subgroups. Change processes need to be designed to harness these forces for creating and supporting change. *As forces already in existence, they must first be made pliable, then altered or shifted, and finally made stable again to support the change.*

3. Essentially, unilateral power and authority structures underlie the hierarchical ordering of organizational roles. *Expectations of the superior are therefore more important forces for creating change in an individual than the expectations of his subordinates.* Also, those with a direct authority relationship—line superiors—have more influence than those without direct authority—staff trainers.

[18] Milton Hall, "Supervising People—Closing the Gap Between What We Think and What We Do," *Advanced Management,* XII (September 1947), pp. 129-135.

4. The attitudes, beliefs, and values of an individual are more firmly grounded in the groups which have continuing psychological meaning to him than in those where he has only temporary membership. The supervisor's role of interlocking the activities of two organizational units requires that he have continuing membership in two groups: (a) the organizational unit directed by his superior in which he is a subordinate along with his immediate peers; and (b) the organizational unit for which he is responsible. *Change processes designed to work with individual supervisors off the job in temporarily created training groups contain less force for initiating and reinforcing change than those which work with an individual in situ.*

5. Information about the functioning of a system may introduce a need for change. This is especially true when the new data are seen as objective and at variance with common perceptions and expectations. Change processes organized around objective, new social facts about one's own organizational situation have more force for change than those organized around general principles about human behavior. *The more meaningful and relevant the material, the greater the likelihood of change.*

6. Involvement and participation in the planning, collection, analysis, and interpretation of information initiate powerful forces for change. Own facts are better understood, more emotionally acceptable, and more likely to be utilized than those of some "outside expert." *Participation in analysis and interpretation helps by-pass those resistances which arise from proceeding too rapidly or too slowly.*

7. Objective information on direction and magnitude of change—knowledge of results—facilitates further improvement. *Change processes which furnish adequate knowledge on progress and specify criteria against which to measure improvement are apt to be more successful in creating and maintaining change than those which do not.*

COMPARISON OF "CLASSROOM" HUMAN RELATIONS TRAINING AND ORGANIZATIONAL FEEDBACK

This is only a partial listing of the points with which a scientifically based technology of social change in organizational settings will have to be concerned. Our conceptualization and the identification of the relevant individual and organizational variables and their interrelationship is at a primitive stage. The systematic quantitative investigation of the effectiveness of different change procedures has scarcely begun. Even at this early date, however, a comparison between the structure and process of feedback and "classroom" human relations training as two different types of change procedures may be a useful exercise. It may help identify variables or facets of change processes which merit greater experimentation and investigation both by the practitioners and by those researchers interested in organizational change. By a "classroom" human relations program we mean a training which would consist of a series of classroom-like meetings in which supervisors from many different points of the organization meet to listen to a presentation of psychological principles which a trainer from the personnel department thinks they ought to know about and be ready to use on the job after a brief discussion following the training. This kind of training experience differs from the feedback process in a number of respects. These differences are stated to keep the comparisons reasonably brief and to sharpen the contrasts.

1. What are the objectives?

"Classroom" Training—Improve supervisor-subordinate relations through changing the supervisors' understanding of human behavior, attitudes, and skills.

Organizational Feedback—Improve organizational functioning through changing understanding, attitudes, and behavior among all members of the organization.

2. What is the setting in which change is being attempted?

"Classroom" Training—Trainees are taken off the job and out of the network of interpersonal relationships in which they normally function for training in an "encapsulated"[19] classroom-like situation.

Organizational Feedback—Change is attempted as a regular part of the day's work in established organizational relationships.

3. What is the informational content?

"Classroom" Training—General psychological principles of human behavior, case materials, or data from outside the training group and often the organization, only occasionally using problems from the group's own experience.

Organizational Feedback—Objective quantitative information about attitudes, beliefs, and expectations of the trainees themselves, or the subordinates in their own organization.

4. What is the method?

"Classroom" Training—Lectures, presentations, films, skits, and occasionally role-playing followed by discussion on how to apply what has been learned back on the job.

[19] M. Haire, "Some Problems of Industrial Training," *Journal of Social Issues*, IV, No. 3 (1948), pp. 41-47.

Organizational Feedback—The progressive introduction of new information about the problems within the groups for which the trainees are responsible. Group discussions of the meaning and action implications of the findings, followed by group decisions on next steps for changing or handling the situation.

5. Who are the trainees?

"Classroom" Training—First-line supervisors and foremen whose superiors may have, but more often have not, had the course.

Organizational Feedback—Everyone in the organization from the top down[20]—the president, top management, intermediate and first-line supervision, *and* employees.

6. What is the training unit?

"Classroom" Training—An aggregate or collection of individual supervisors from different departments throughout the organization. A functional conglomerate without continuing psychological meaning for the individuals. Frequently seen as a "group" simply because the individuals are in close spatial proximity to one another.

Organizational Feedback—An organizational unit whose members have an organizational function to perform and whose members (a superior and his immediate subordinates) have continuing psychological meaning perceptually and behaviorally to one another as a team or family.

7. Who is the change agent?

"Classroom" Training—An outsider—an expert, a staff man—who has no direct, continuing authority or power over the trainee and few recurrent opportunities to reinforce the training.

Organizational Feedback—The organizational unit's line supervisor, who is given some help through pre- and post-meeting coaching by the expert outsider.

8. How is the pace or rate of change set?

"Classroom" Training—The trainer sets the pace, attempting to gear the training to average trainee's ability to comprehend and assimilate the material.

Organizational Feedback—The members of the group move from one topic to another as they are ready for the next step.

9. How long does the change process continue?

"Classroom" Training—A fixed number of days or weeks, seldom less than 16 or more than 80 hours.

Organizational Feedback—No fixed length of time, the change procedure usually continues over a period of months—6 to 24 months.

[20] N. R. F. Maier, "A Human Relations Program for Supervision," *Industrial and Labor Relations Review,* I (April 1948), pp. 443-464.

10. How much tension is there?

"Classroom" Training—Usually relatively little, most trainees feel they already know a good deal about human behavior and how others feel.

Organizational Feedback—Frequently considerable, as objective information and particularly the differences between supervisory beliefs and practices come into a focus so sharp that complacency is shattered and the security about what is social reality is shaken.

11. What assumptions are made about attitudes and how they are changed?[21]

"Classroom" Training—The primary assumption is that the trainee does not know certain facts, that his previous organization of relevant information will be altered when he understands the new facts. Attitudes are seen as a function of the range of information available to the trainee; they are changed by altering cognitive structure.

Organizational Feedback—Here the assumptions are that the trainee already has satisfying ways of seeing things and relating to others, that attitudes and behavior can be changed only by altering their motivational bases. Norms of psychologically relevant groups are seen as more important determinants of attitudes than cognitive processes.

12. How is effectiveness of the change measured?

"Classroom" Training—Usually by informal comments of trainees, occasionally by interviews or questionnaires with the trainees after the training.

Organizational Feedback—By changes in employees' perception of their supervisor's behavior.

The differences drawn between these two types of procedures for creating change in an organizational setting may not be as marked as presented here. Human relations training programs do vary tremendously from company to company and from time to time. There is no single pattern. Since we know little about the frequency of different species of human relations training programs, the specific mix of content, method, setting, etc., which we used as the basis of our contrast may no longer be found in organizations. Our comparison aimed to emphasize the extent to which various characteristics of change processes vary on the basic dimension of *motivation for change.*

Different contents, different methods, different settings, different training units, and different change agents contain different moti-

[21] I. Sarnoff and D. Katz, "The Motivational Bases of Attitude Change," *Journal of Abnormal and Social Psychology,* XLIX (January 1954), pp. 115-124.

vational impacts for change. What constitutes the most effective combination for changing behavior in organizations is not known. Few practitioners have really done any bold experimenting; almost none have combined measurement and experimenting to search for the most significant dimensions and variables in change processes. This is an area in which there is a great need for social experimentation and social invention.

In the social sciences, as in the physical sciences, invention plays a crucial role. Inventions in social technology—skills and processes for creating change—and innovations in measurement both contribute speedily to progress in understanding social phenomena. The responsibility of experimenting with different methods of measuring change and with new procedures for investigating the interrelationship of functioning organizational processes rests heavily with the students of social organization. The rate at which knowledge about organization is developed will probably be closely correlated to the rate at which we try new approaches to the study of problems in this area.

PART IV

TRADE UNIONS

· XI ·

THE IMPACT OF THE UNION ON THE MANAGEMENT ORGANIZATION

BY WILLIAM FOOTE WHYTE
Cornell University

GROWTH OF THE INDUSTRIAL RELATIONS DEPARTMENT

The industrial relations department is one of the union's chief contributions to the management organization. Even some of these departments in nonunion companies must be considered in large measure a response to the push of unionization. There were specialized industrial relations functionaries in the mass production industries before the advent of unions, but in most cases their activities in the twenties and early thirties were confined to the process of initial employment.

By the 1940's, industrial relations activities had expanded greatly, and the top man now generally carried the title of manager of industrial relations or of employee relations or personnel. He was still outranked by the vice presidents of sales, engineering, manufacturing, and so on. By the 1950's, in most large companies the top industrial relations man had attained the rank of vice president.

The union created an obvious need for the development of negotiators within the industrial relations department. In some companies with many plants and many different contracts, a group of men can spend all of their time throughout the year in preparing for negotiations and in negotiating contracts. But this is not all. Unions create other needs involved in the day-to-day administration of the work force.

Unions have weakened the workers' dependent relationship upon management. Years ago, many management people prided themselves upon taking a personal interest in the welfare of their workers. This meant that they might grant special consideration to workers beset with personal difficulties or unable by reason of health or age to carry on their regular jobs. But these favors were generally based as much upon attitude toward management as upon need. The "loyal" employee might expect to be "taken care of," whereas there would be no favors for the "troublemaker."

Union pressure has generally put an end to this sort of situation. Unions insist that what a man receives in pay, in hospitalization benefits, in his retirement plan, and so on, shall not be subject to the discretion of management, but shall be determined by policies established to some degree through contract negotiations.

On all fronts, the union has demanded standardization, and management has had to hire specialists and develop special activities in order to meet these demands.

To justify its wage and promotion system, management has had to develop procedures for job descriptions and job evaluation. Taylor's scientific management movement began such activity before large scale unionization, but it was immensely stimulated by union pressure.

Unions have exercised heavy pressure through the grievance procedure on matters of discipline and promotion. This has led not only to the creation of a set of functionaries to deal with the union on grievance procedure, but also to efforts to standardize management's policies and to build up the necessary paper records for dealing with the union.

In the past, management has claimed the right to promote the ablest individual, regardless of seniority. But how is ability to be determined? Before unionization, in some cases, promotions simply went to the workers who were able to ingratiate themselves with the foreman. Such favoritism accounts for much of the union pressure to establish seniority as a basis for promotion. Even before unionization, many managements followed seniority in promotion in most cases, and today most managements seem willing to promote by seniority in relatively unskilled jobs. However, most managements seek to retain the right to consider ability on skilled jobs. In some cases, unions are willing to agree to this in principle, but they demand proof of relative qualifications. This has forced management to examine its jobs carefully and to keep more adequate records upon the performance of individual workers.

Unionization frequently released a flood of grievances and complaints against foremen. Often this led higher management people to see the foreman as a scapegoat for all the ills of worker-management relations. If this were true, then something had to be done to train the foreman to establish better human relations with his workers. This interest led to the widespread development of training programs in American industry. The union influence did not stop at this point, for, as the more sophisticated management people began to recognize that some of the problems had their roots above the foreman level, the emphasis in training shifted toward higher levels in the organization.

Union pressure for fringe benefits created a need for a new type of specialist within the industrial relations organization: a man who knew something about principles of insurance and actuarial problems.

These new activities have led to a professionalization of the personnel field. In making its first response to the union, management often looked toward some individual whose sole or main qualification was that he got along well with people. Such an individual may find favor with workers and union officials at the outset, but management soon finds that just "knowing how to get along with people" is not enough. Including as it does contract negotiation, wage and salary administration, selection and employment, safety, merit rating, job description, job evaluation, grievance handling, training, benefit programs, and so on, the field of industrial relations has become highly technical. The industrial relations administrator does not need to know the technical details in all of these areas, but he must have a general familiarity with them sufficient to know when his subordinates are talking sense or nonsense. Furthermore, the stakes in industrial relations have become so high that management cannot tolerate the well meaning bungler who merely happens to "like people."

We now have college and graduate school programs designed to train men in industrial relations. and industrial relations men in industry are seeking to enhance the standing of their field through clothing it with professional regalia. While this urge toward professionalization may have some roots in a desire to add to the prestige of the field, nevertheless the job functions have become sufficiently technical and specialized to lead naturally in the direction of professionalization.

While noting the influence of unions, we should not think in terms of a simple cause-effect relationship. Before the advent of unions, there were people in management who would have liked to develop an improved human relations program but found themselves blocked by management's preoccupation with the "practical" matters of costs, technology, etc. Possible slowdowns and strikes being matters of obvious practical concern, unions have greatly strengthened the hand of many people who were privately (but ineffectually) committed to a broader social viewpoint.

Unions and Centralization

Unionization has also been a strong influence toward centralization of decision-making in management. Before unions, in many companies, the foreman was almost an autonomous manager of his shop. He hired anybody he pleased, and he did his firing with equal freedom.

A first move on the part of a union is to seek to limit this freedom of discharge. Faced with a flood of grievances, management cannot any longer leave this matter in the hands of the foreman. The foreman may still be able to initiate the steps that lead to a discharge, but he is carefully coached on his rights and obligations under the contract and under management policies. Furthermore, he is expected to consult with higher line management or the industrial relations department on all but the most clear-cut cases.

The contract will state that the union steward or the worker or both shall seek to resolve a grievance with the foreman before passing it up to higher management. We find, however, that in most cases the foreman has very little freedom in this area. Management recognizes that a decision in one department can be used by the union as a precedent to justify a grievance in another department. Thus all grievances have at least a potential plant-wide impact. Management is therefore inclined to exercise supervision or control over the foreman on this point.

This centralization takes place not only at the plant level but also at higher levels. Even where the multiplant company does not have a company-wide contract with a union, management recognizes that a collective bargaining or grievance decision in one plant can be used by the union to exert pressure in other plants. Where management and union have worked out a company-wide contract, with arbitration as the final grievance step, the centralizing effect is still greater.

The growth of large scale unionism and company-wide bargaining has led some students to believe that all the really important union-management decisions affecting life in the plant are taken at a level far above the plant. They suggest that those who spend their time making case studies of plants are not studying important problems.

Certainly we mislead ourselves if we assume that the plant of a large corporation and the local union of a large international are autonomous social systems. On the other hand, we are equally naïve if we assume that the top level industrial relations decisions are the only or even the most important determinants of union-management behavior in the plant. Certain points, such as wage rates, may of course be decided at the top and imposed uniformly. However, as Melville Dalton[1] has shown, the local plant has a life of its own, influenced, to be sure, by top level action, but not completely dominated from above.

In Dalton's case study, both local management and local union were presumably bound by a company-wide contract. Nevertheless, Dalton observed that the actual day-to-day handling of union-management problems often involved agreements that were not included in the contract or were actually in violation of certain clauses. He found that local people on both sides had pressing local problems to meet and, in meeting them, they tended to develop an exchange of favors. There was just one limitation; the grievances and other matters discussed were not put in writing. It was only when one or both parties wished the matter to come to the attention of higher officials that the grievance would be put in writing and processed through the formally prescribed channels. By handling matters informally, local plant and union officials were able both to adjust to

[1] "Unofficial Union-Management Relations," in Robert Dubin, *Human Relations in Administration* (New York: Prentice-Hall, 1951).

their problems and to maintain a considerable degree of independence from controls from above the plant level. Thus we have formal rigidity balanced by informal flexibility.

Management Prerogatives and Union Participation[2]

The union necessarily represents a challenge to management's unilateral control. The very existence of the union raises far-reaching questions regarding the nature, extent, and limitations of management's authority.

The prerogative problem may first come to an issue in the establishment of the grievance procedure. Recognizing that day-to-day management decisions can have the effect of nullifying some clauses of the contract, a union demands that the grievances it raises on these issues be allowed to go to an impartial arbitrator for decision. Historically management has looked upon such a provision as an abdication of management's authority. In effect, the union is proposing that important policy questions be decided by someone outside.

In early years, managements were inclined to resist vigorously such a surrender of powers. Today it is taken for granted by most managements that there shall be provision for arbitration of grievances involving the interpretation of the contract. This change in point of view probably has two main causes.

In the first place, management learned that the union did have the power to challenge management's decisions even without an arbitration clause. The slowdown weapon could readily be used. In extreme cases, the union could organize a departmental or even a plant-wide strike to support its grievances. No union was willing to sign a no-strike agreement during the course of a contract period unless it also won a provision for arbitration of grievances. Thus arbitration became a price management generally agreed to pay in return for achieving some stability and predictability in its industrial relations.

In the second place, arbitration has become so generally accepted on the American industrial relations scene that any management

[2] Neil W. Chamberlain, *The Union Challenge to Management Control* (New York: Harper, 1948). This is the best and most comprehensive statement of the union's impact upon management.

which now refuses such a provision would put itself in a very unfavorable light with its employees and the general public.

The establishment of arbitration provides the union with a good deal of security but does not determine the extent of the union's participation in activities that had previously been reserved entirely to management. What role is the union to play now?

According to one management theory, the union should be confined to the role of a watchdog over the provisions of the contract. The objective here is to have the union speak to management only when it claims that a clause in the contract has been violated. Otherwise management is to operate the plant as if the union as an organization did not exist. With this approach, the hope is that management will be able to do a good enough job in abiding by the contract so that the union stewards and officers will not bother management very much. Such a management approach puts the union in a position where it can only discuss problems with management by challenging a decision management has already made. It naturally leads the union officers to search for any excuse that will justify a charge of a contract violation. With this type of relationship, the union is constantly in a position of trying to initiate activity for management while management exercises no initiative in the situation and can only seek to hold a strong defensive position.

In the course of time the watchdog relationship becomes transformed in most cases. As management people become accustomed to dealing with union officers, it becomes difficult for them to maintain a strict legalistic position that prohibits discussion of anything but grievances. The management people in the plant like to think of themselves as practical men, and they come to recognize that the strictly legalistic approach leaves many practical problems unresolved. Thus the union's participation tends to increase, but there still remains a question as to the areas in which the union shall be permitted or encouraged to participate.

A union's participation (beyond that achieved in the grievance procedure) is extended most readily in those areas which are far removed from the production process. This may happen first in community welfare activities such as drives for the Red Cross and the Community Fund, where unions have demanded some part in and recognition for the contribution made by workers. They have been able to win participation by advising their members to refuse to cooperate in drives conducted by management alone. These activities of local union leaders have helped to establish them as important community figures. This acceptance in community-wide welfare activities has also established a different kind of personal contact between themselves and management people which may, in turn, influence relationships back in the plant.[3]

There are other plant activities that are relatively easy for the union to penetrate. The union may make an issue of the quality of food or the prices charged in the plant cafeteria. Since people naturally have a tendency to pour out all sorts of dissatisfactions in ostensible complaints about food, this issue can be argued forever. Management is likely to get tired of cafeteria arguments and to think that the pressure of complaints can only be reduced if the union itself takes some responsibility for the cafeteria. In most cases plant cafeterias are not operated by management directly but are under contract to a concessionaire. This makes it easier for management to stand aside, almost in the role of an impartial third party, and allow the development of a union committee which will discuss cafeteria problems with the concessionaire.

Management likewise finds it difficult to resist union demands for participation in safety committees. It is hard to stand on prerogatives when union officers argue that the lives of their members are at stake.

Even if management, allowing participation in the activities so far discussed, still stands firmly against permitting its extension into production matters, the initial participation tends to lead to more participation. As management people learn to work together with union people on one set of problems, they may find themselves informally discussing other problems in spite of themselves.

Many management people recognize that involving the union officers in discussion of problems makes for a more harmonious union-management relationship. They are determined, however, that the union officers get the satisfactions of participation from areas not directly connected with production. Generally the union officers are not satisfied with such halfway measures. They feel that

[3] Mark Starr, "Role of Union Organization," *Industry and Society,* William F. Whyte, ed. (New York: McGraw-Hill, 1946).

a little participation is better than none at all, but they recognize that so far they are just participating on the fringes. They know as well as does management that the purpose of the plant is production and that what happens in the production process has the most vital effects upon them and their members. They are then naturally inclined to push to extend participation into this area.

In some cases, participation has been extended into the area of the production process—sometimes with mutually satisfactory results, sometimes not. It is not my purpose to discuss the conditions necessary in order to make such participation mutually satisfying. I am only pointing out that such an extension of union participation introduces basic changes in the functioning of the management organization.

Without a union, management does not have to respond to complaints and suggestions from below. Under the union watchdog relationship, it is the union which is constantly seeking to initiate activity for management. Management responds or fails to respond but never itself seeks to initiate activity directly for the union in turn. As union-management participation grows, management increasingly takes the initiative in its dealings with the union. It channels information to employees through the union. It also calls upon union officers for help in solving certain production and discipline problems. Now management has two channels through which to initiate activity toward its employees instead of just the line organization which was previously used.

Instead of announcing its decisions and then preparing to defend them against union challenges, the management incorporates union officers in the actual decision-making process. This may be done on a wide variety of problems beyond contract negotiation, which is, by necessity, a joint decision-making process. The union thus moves from the role of watchdog to that of participant. This involves a far-reaching change in the pattern of human relations and in the organization of management activities.

There must be widely differing types of participation arrangements between union and management, each of them having a different impact upon the functioning of the management organization. Research so far has simply shown the possibilities of establishing some sort of participation arrangement. We have not yet had research directed toward determining exactly how a given union and management function under a given sort of arrangement.

CONCLUDING QUESTIONS

In many companies, most of the activities of the industrial relations department today are, directly and indirectly, a reaction to unionization. In many cases these activities have been developed for the purpose of meeting union challenges and preventing the union from making further extensions of control.

This process began when unions were looked upon as interlopers in the province of management. The activities were essentially defensive in character. Today in most companies management's attitude toward unions has changed. Few managers are enthusiastic believers in unions, but most of them have come to accept the union as an integral part of the social system of the plant.

From this point of view, it follows that an industrial relations program based entirely upon a *defensive* philosophy is no longer appropriate. A new philosophy, based upon the full gamut of contacts and interactions between union and management, in which their coexistence in a single social system is the center of attention, is just beginning to develop. What implications does such a new philosophy have for the redirection of industrial relations programs?

While industrial relations departments have grown in size and prestige in response to unionization, generally they have been preoccupied with developing strategies and procedures to meet the union challenge on a piecemeal basis. Often the operation of such systems and procedures becomes so absorbing of time and energy that the personnel man is unable to search for the underlying human problems. The personnel man calls himself an advisor to line management on its human problems, but in most cases little time is spent upon such consultation. In the past, he was only called upon for advice at a time when something had gone wrong, when it was already too late to work out a very constructive solution to the problem. Now he is beginning to be called on before the crisis so that he has an opportunity to apply some preventive social medicine. This represents a sharp departure from past practice. It involves redefining of the personnel man's role in management, rising above the comfortable security of present strategies and procedures, and learning new skills of social diagnosis, consultation, and action. Will he be able to meet this challenge?

The union's influence upon management centralization provides us with our final question.

Human relations research has amply demonstrated that people are more satisfied with solutions to their problems if they themselves have an opportunity to participate in reaching those solutions. This argues for local problem solving.

But if the union has only the power, in dealing with a large corporation, to shut down one plant at one time, then it has little bargaining strength. These union needs clearly call for a company-wide approach.

Dalton has shown that people will work out local adaptations even under a company-wide contract. But these result in undercover arrangements. Here the higher level union and management officials necessarily act upon fictitious assumptions regarding the nature of union-management relations at the plant level.

This sort of adaptation is certainly better than complete rigidity, but it hardly seems a good solution to the problem. Can we not devise better ways to reconcile local adaptations with large scale agreements? Can we invent or evolve a better federal form for union and management?

· XII ·

INTERPERSONAL RELATIONS IN COLLECTIVE BARGAINING

MASON HAIRE
University of California

Interactions between people depend first on the perceptions, by the parties involved, of the situation and of self and other. The perceptual process is a highly active one of selecting, organizing, and distorting in an attempt to make sense of a bewildering array of ambiguous stimuli. The end product tends to be a coherent picture, but it is not necessarily a veridical one. Behavior, however, tends to follow the perception rather than the reality, and consequently, in considering interactive behavior, it behooves us to examine this process of perception. Labor-management relations and, specifically, collective bargaining are not exceptions to this general principle.

In many cases in the social sciences we seem to have overobjectified variables which are essentially subjective. Thus, we often speak of institutional structures like labor and management, meaning them to be many-faceted institutions with long histories, complex causes and internal dynamics. This much is true, as long as we are content to speak as sociologists or as historians. But, when we speak as analyzers of the causes of behavior, these institutions do not necessarily have any psychological reality for the individual. To understand the individual's behavior, we must first know what it looks like to him. This is the kind of thing that the psychologist calls a henomenological analysis.[1] It proposes to ask first, simply "What ; there?" in the world of experience of the subject concerned. It ttempts to build an explanation of behavior on this kind of psy-hologically conceived base of experience rather than on a logically onceived base of inference. It is essentially an attempt to work from ıside out.

This chapter then will consider how we organize our perceptions f other people, how these become role perceptions in situations, ow these role perceptions influence interaction, and finally, what /e know about role perceptions in labor-management interaction.

THE PERCEPTION OF PEOPLE AS A PROBLEM-SOLVING PROCESS

'actors Influencing the Perceptual Organization

It is a cliche in perception to say that we do not perceive what ; "out there." Yet it is a truism that needs to be repeated, because ıany of our perceptions have the compelling character, as part of ıe immediate experience, of belonging to the thing out there. If I ›uch my hand with a heated rod, I feel as if the *rod* is warm, al-ıough the warmth belongs to me and not to the rod. The first thing 'e must remember is that many of our experiences carry with them ıe character of seeming to be representations of what is "out there."

The second thing we must remember is that we often add a great eal in the process of organizing and making sense out of the stim-lus data with which we are presented. Many experiments in simple erception have explored the experience of "things" when the hing" has no simple objective reality. Moreover, the organizing of ems into meaningful wholes of this kind can be shown to distort nd select among available stimulus data in the process. Thus, a gray ot seen as a member of a group of yellow dots will be seen to be ellow; seen alone it will look gray. Its experienced character is istorted by its membership in the group in our experience. Both ıe group and the membership in the group are products of the rganism's contribution to the perception rather than of the stim-lus data. Yet these organizational phenomena are powerful deter-

[1] R. B. MacLeod, "The Phenomenological Approach to Social Psychology," *ychological Review,* LIV (July 1947), pp. 193-211.

miners of the shape of experience, and our perception of the item is heavily influenced by them.

What we think of as simple stimulus items that are experienced as "out there" characteristics of the person perceived are neither simple properties of the stimulus object, nor are they undistorted by the process of apprehending them. Consider, for example, the case cited by Asch,[2] who describes a person as "helpful, quick, and clumsy" and another person as "helpful, quick and skillful." The two groups of adjectives are organized immediately into wholes which change the character of the individual items. Even though the word "quick" seems superficially to be a simple identical reference in the two descriptions, we do not perceive it as such. The "quickness" is quite different in one case from the other. Similarly, Haire and Grunes[3] have shown that when we have a well organized perception of a personality, information which is not harmonious with the perception is distorted, ignored, denied, and explained away more often than it is integrated into the perception and allowed to alter the organization.

In addition to these organizational factors which arise from within the stimulus material itself, we can also identify external influences. The perceiver's general attitudes partly determine what he will see. For instance, Stagner[4] asked students to check a list of traits which they saw as characteristic of factory workers. The students who were independently determined to be pro-labor saw the workers as having the same traits as themselves and saw these traits as pleasant —both of these findings to a greater degree than students who were anti-labor. A combination of these two effects—the organizational and the attitudinal—occurs in the "halo" effect or "logical error." Raters tend to operate on the basis of preconceptions about wha

[2] S. E. Asch, "Forming Impressions of Personality," *Journal of Abnormal and Social Psychology*, XLI (July 1946), pp. 258-290.

[3] Mason Haire and Willa F. Grunes, "Perceptual Defenses: Processes Protecting an Organized Perception of Another Personality," *Human Relations*, III (December 1950), pp. 403-412.

[4] Ross Stagner, "Psychological Aspects of Industrial Conflict, I. Perception," *Personnel Psychology*, I (January 1948), pp. 131-144.

[5] E. L. Thorndike, "A Constant Error in Psychological Ratings," *Journal of Applied Psychology*, IV (1920), pp. 25-29; T. Newcomb, "An Experiment Designed to Test the Validity of a Rating Technique," *Journal of Educational Psychology*, XXII (1931), pp. 279-289; J. P. Guilford, *Psychometric Methods* (New York: McGraw-Hill, 1936).

raits go together, and thus a person seen as having one trait tends
o be seen as having certain other characteristics not provided by
he stimulus information.

In general, we tend to overestimate the unity of the personality,
hat is, to tie it together into a well-knit package instead of dealing
vith the objective data which are apt to be contradictory, variable,
nd vague. We not only select and distort our perception to enforce
his organizational nicety, but in interactions with people we tend
o force the other person to produce behaviors which will fit with
ur perception. In any interaction between two people, the actions
f *A* partly define and limit the behaviors of *B*. Sometimes these
orces are grounded in *A*'s personality and sometimes in his position.
'hus the boss, in speaking to his employees, enforces certain limita-
ons of behavior on the other which act to select the kind of infor-
ation about the personality which can be received.

oles as Special Kinds of Organized Perceptions in Dealing with Other Persons

When we interact with other people we usually perceive them not
nly as personalities, but as having positions in which they operate.
ociologists have tended to speak of these coherent patterns of
ehavior as roles. Psychologists seem to modify the usage a little,
utting more emphasis on the coherence and meaning of the pattern
f behaviors for the doer and for the perceiver. In either case it
mounts to the perception of an organized pattern of behaviors,
hether this hanging-togetherness is seen by the role player or the
ther person. Moreover, such a role serves to limit what the person
the role can do, and to engender in the perceivers certain expect-
ncies of what he will do. In this sense, the role serves to do more
han the simple organization of perception spoken of above. It
ntegrates the personality into the situation, partly sets the character
f the interaction, and allows some predictions about future be-
avior.

nteraction Depends on Role Perceptions

So far the experimental examples of perceptual distortion have
een illustrated only in the response of seeing. To relate this concept
interaction among people, it is necessary to demonstrate that be-

havior follows these experienced patterns in the apprehension o
other personalities. An ingenious experiment provides this bridge
Several classes of students were asked to describe the personality o
a new instructor. Half the students were told he was considered b
his friends to be a "rather cold person, industrious, critical, prac
tical, and determined." The other half were told he was considere
by his friends to be a "very warm person, industrious, critical, prac
tical, and determined." All the students thought they had the sam
description and were acting on the basis of the same informatio

After the class they described his behavior. The "warm" grou
found him considerate, good natured, sociable, and informal. Th
"cold" group saw him as self-centered, unsociable, irritable, an
formal. Clearly, as before, the single stimulus item has altered th
general perceptual organization of the personality. But, more im
portant for our present purpose, it was also possible in this exper
ment to get information on interaction. Classroom participation wa
observed and recorded, and it was found that 56 per cent of th
"warm" subjects entered the discussion, whereas only 32 per cen
of the "cold" subjects did so. Since the warm-cold descriptio
were provided randomly to alternate students, the difference
behavior seems attributable to the difference in perception. A
though the leader's behavior was identical to both groups, the soci
perception served to determine the person's behavior in interactio
Here the organized perception is of an individual, influenced by
description. Just such an organization of perceptions occurs in th
case of an organization or of an individual seen in the role of a
organization member.

ROLE PERCEPTIONS AND INTERACTION IN LABOR-MANAGEMENT RELATIONS

Distortion and Selection in Labor-Management Role Perceptions

One might expect the kind of phenomena we have just describe
in the perception of one another by representatives of labor an
management. Here we have all the factors: a bewildering array
ambiguous stimuli presented by the behavior of each, strong mo

[6] H. H. Kelley, "The Warm-Cold Variable in First Impressions of Personality
Journal of Abnormal and Social Psychology, XVIII (April 1950), pp. 431-4

ational forces connected with each one's perception of the other, and ighly charged interactions following on these perceptions. Both asual and more systematic observation of the two parties suggests ıat such misperceptions do in fact occur, and indeed, Gruen[7] suggests that, in the studies of industrial peace conducted by the Na- onal Planning Association, "good relations were accompanied by hanges in perception of role on the side of both management and ıe union from the traditional role and from the roles still preval- nt in much of Europe." Paster[8] uses the same kind of concept in iscussing the mediation process. The more or less self-conscious osturing for effect in the relationship is an attempt to structure the ɔle perception of the other, and Paster points to such stock roles s "the threatened departure" and "the temper tantrum" as part of ıe repertoire of the parties.

More systematic observation strengthens the conclusion. Rem- ıers and Remmers[9] conducted an experiment designed to see how vorkers and management perceive one another's positions regarding upervision. The results showed that labor considerably underesti- ıated the actual goodness of performance of management on the est of supervision, and that, on the other hand, management sig- ificantly overestimated labor leaders' performance. When one re- ıembers that the two parties will be talking to one another about vents of supervision and basing their statements and arguments n what each *thinks* the other believes about supervision, it is clear ıat there is room for considerable error in the interaction.

In another empirical study, Haire[10] obtained a more direct meas- re of labor and management's perceptions of one another. Repre-

[7] Walter Gruen, "Dual Allegiance to Union and Management, (A Sym- osium), 5. A Theoretical Examination of the Concept of Dual Allegiance," *ersonnel Psychology*, VII (July 1954), pp. 72-80.

[8] Irving Paster, "Psychological Factors in Industrial Mediation," *Personnel*, XXI (1954), pp. 115-127.

[9] L. J. Remmers and H. H. Remmers, "Studies in Industrial Empathy; I. abor Leaders' Attitudes Toward Industrial Supervision and Their Estimate f Management's Attitude," *Personnel Psychology*, II (1949), pp. 427-436; E. G. Ɨiller and H. H. Remmers, "Studies in Industrial Empathy, II. Management's ttitudes Toward Industrial Supervision and Their Estimates of Labor Atti- ıdes," *Personnel Psychology*, III (1950), pp. 33-40.

[10] Mason Haire, "Role Perceptions in Labor-Management Relations: An xperimental Approach," *Industrial and Labor Relations Review*, VIII (January 955), pp. 204-216.

sentatives of both groups were asked to describe the personality o a man whose picture they saw and of whom they had a brief de scription. Half of each group was told he was a union leader and half that he was a management representative. Thus each group described their perception of a representative of each, permitting full comparison of the perceptions. They saw very different things A simple table will illustrate the difference. In describing a *single man,* the four perceptions were:

Management sees A as a management man	Management sees A as a union man	Labor sees A as a management man	Labor sees A as a union man
He is	He is	He is	He is
honest	alert	active	active
conscientious	determined	aggressive	alert
adaptable	aggressive	alert	capable

They hardly seem like the same man. Other analyses of Haire's data showed, for instance, that each group felt that it was dependable and the other group less so; each group felt that its representatives saw the others' problems, but that the other group did not; and each group saw itself but not the other as characterized by skill in thinking and interpersonal relations.

In another aspect of the same study, Haire showed, by an interaction content analysis of verbatim transcripts of labor-management negotiations, that patterned behavior tendencies characteristic of each group could be identified. This method of analysis offers a method for objective, empirical, and reliable description of the interaction patterns in bargaining conference.

The Effect on an Actor of Another's Role Perception

All of us, in face-to-face behavior, are more or less conscious of the way in which we are seen, and often we spend a good deal of time in interaction in attempts to correct what we believe to be the way in which the other person sees us. Some evidence of this kind of perception of the other's perception of self in labor-management relations is available. In Haire's study mentioned above, it was clear, for example, that both labor and management were aware of the fact that they were attacked on specific grounds; each defended himself chiefly (though not entirely) on the grounds on which he was attacked. A more significant bit of evidence of labor's perception of the role management sees for labor lies in the fact that labor defended its status and power many times before it had ever been attacked. Long term aspects of the relationship and stereotypical role perceptions seem to have determined a set of interaction items which, at best, wasted the time of the negotiation and perhaps also engendered emotional responses which hindered final solutions.

On the more positive side, Nagle[11] showed the beneficial effect of this recognition of the way one is seen by another. He used two questionnaires designed to show the way the employee saw his supervisor and the way he saw the company and plant management. He was able to show that the more sensitive the supervisor is to the employee's attitude toward him, the more favorable the employee tends to be toward him, and also the more sensitive the supervisor is to the employee's attitude toward him, the more favorable the employee tends to be toward the plant and the management. It might be suggested, however, that if the supervisor saw in the employee's role perception something which was totally unacceptable to him, the heightened sensitivity might have been a source of immediate conflict. However, even in this case, the more accurate the perception of role incompatibility, the more likely the conflict is to be eventually resolved.

Stagner's[12] studies of dual allegiance also cast encouraging light on the bilaterality of this perception of self and other. He found that a dual allegiance among rank and file to union and management was not only possible, but characteristic of the plants studied. Where the worker found a role in relation to each institution where his need-satisfaction was greater than deprivation or frustration, he tended to be favorable to both. The role perception of self as "union man . . . company man" does not seem to be on a single con-

[11] Bryant F. Nagle, "Productivity, Employee Attitude and Supervisor Sensitivity," *Personnel Psychology*, VII (1954), pp. 219-232.

[12] Ross Stagner, "Dual Allegiance to Union and Management (A Symposium), I. Dual Allegiance as a Problem in Modern Society," *Personnel Psychology*, VII (July 1954), pp. 41-47.

tinuum, but seems to be psychologically separate, so that each, o
both, can be maximized or minimized at once.

ROLE COMPATIBILITY IN FRUITFUL RELATIONSHIPS

What can we say in summary of this approach through the prob
lem of role perceptions? It seems possible to say, as a genera
description of harmonious and fruitful relationships, that:

1. *A* must see in the situation and in the relationship a role for him
self which he can accept.
2. *A* must feel that he is allowed to play this role. That is, *A* must se
B as seeing the role for *A* which *A* sees for himself, and *A* must see *B*'
behavior as making *A*'s role possible.
3. *A* must see a role for *B* which he, *A*, can accept.
4. *A* must see *B* as accepting this role.
5. All of these points must be true, conversely, for *B*.

At first glance this seems to be an incredibly complex way of statin
a simple relationship between two people. On the other hand, i
seems to fit a wide variety of successful relationships. When n
real role compatibility is achieved, either *A* or *B* or both will try t
change the role perceptions of the other and hence the terms of th
relationship. Failing that, either or both of them may resort to som
form of violence to change the relationship—a strike, a "scene,"
threat of divorce, or whatever is appropriate to the situation. I
violence is seen as maladaptive, either may withdraw from the rela
tionship, or, if one or both can't afford to withdraw physically, h
may withdraw psychologically by reducing his personal commit
ment to the relationship. Any of these results, short of real compati
bility of role perceptions, seems likely to be less than maximall
fruitful.

What have we gained by this apparently circumlocutory restate
ment of the problem? We have known for a long time that if unio
and management leaders can't agree on a contract clause, they wi
try to change the other's behavior with respect to it, and, failin
that, will threaten retaliatory action. If nothing more than this i
said, we have added little. However, considerably more than thi
seems to be implied. In the first place, such a statement puts th
interaction between labor and management in a class with a larg
group of other relationships, makes it amenable to study in the sam

terms, and allows us to use insights gained from the one in the analysis of the others. Further, it repositions the economic issues until they became one of a class of aspects of the position of each party rather than being the sole determinant of the behavior in the relationship. In specific instances, the various aspects will have to be assigned weights, and the economic factor, being a crucial one in the objectives of the relationship, will always be weighted heavily, but not necessarily exclusively. Finally, the restatement of these factors in the relationship in terms of the perception of the two parties helps us to see that any one of them must be dealt with in terms of the way it is seen by one of the members. We are led away from the overobjectivity that has sometimes confused us, and tend to see the reality, in terms of its influence on behavior, of the individual's view of the situation rather than to focus on the facts which we, as outsiders, may know to be true. The additional fact that the whole class of problems, as well as the labor-management problem specifically, has been shown to be susceptible to empirical research on the level of the role-perceptions and interactions of the parties leads us to hope for general statements approaching understanding.

· XIII ·

HUMAN RELATIONS IN THE TRADE UNIONS

BY SOLOMON BARKIN
Textile Workers Union of America

The study of human relations in the trade union is essentially different from that of the business enterprise. The latter is basically a hierarchical, authoritarian, centrally-governed institution, responsive to its fundamental objectives of efficient production and profit. Its focus is on financial rewards to owners, management, and employees. It looks to understand its personnel primarily for guidance on how better to secure its goals and gain employee acceptance of its logics.

The trade union, on the other hand, is a membership organization dedicated to its own constituents' objectives. Its administration is essentially democratic in form. Its purpose is to provide workers with a means for bargaining for better terms of employment, greater security, and rights within the plant. It is a tool for gaining greater personal opportunity, correcting unsavory, irritating, and debilitating conditions, and combating repressive forces in the plant and society. The study of human relations in trade unions centers on the degree of satisfaction its gains provide, the adequacy of its techniques, and the sufficiency of its own institutional activities in meeting member longings and values.

It is in the operation of the union as an institution that a comparison with the business enterprise is more nearly possible. But here again, the membership character of the organization, its democratic structural forms, and the fact that leaders are elected militate against too close a parallel being drawn between their human relations problems. While the business executive's skill is directed toward gaining acceptance of his authority, the union leader's is aimed at effective persuasion. No matter whom the business executive consults or how much advice he receives, he is the final arbiter and his determination is binding. Implementation must be secured through his ultimate authority. On the other hand, no matter how much the union leader short cuts the processes of consultation or formal membership direction, he can never escape them. He is most effective when he molds the instructions given him rather than forces the substitution of his will for that of his following. He can administer the union smoothly when he obtains membership acceptance and endorsement for his decisions and their implementation by the people.

The problems of persuasion are essentially different from those of gaining acceptance of authority. Problems of communication exist in each case, but the tools, procedures, and end results are vastly different. One area of special interest in the study of trade union leadership is the degree to which it observes this distinction and avoids the use of authority and coercion in directing the membership. Where misuse of power exists, the very nature of the institution is violated.[1]

Thus, it is clear that human relations conclusions based only on studies of management cannot be presumed to apply also to unions. An examination of the goals, structure, and programs of unions and of the attitudes and actions of members and leaders provides a framework for a constructive human relations analysis of unions themselves.

SATISFYING THE WORKERS' LONGINGS AND VALUES

Before unions are established, workers ordinarily form social groups within the plants, independent of the functional work arrangements presented by management. These are usually based on

[1] Both the union leader and the business manager are in positions of trust. Either may be tempted to abuse this trust for personal advantage or indulgence, sometimes at the expense of the membership or organization. But the union code demands more self-effacing devotion and avoidance of personal gain. The basic ethics are stricter. Yet the problems of enforcement are similar and both union and business have been lax in pursuing them.

location, prestige, or ethnic, religious, color, age, sex, or job ties. They have at best served as means of communication, establishing social relations or codes, and as vehicles for occasional protests. Seldom have they been the instruments for the continued relief of worker frustration. Even when not in conflict with management, informal groups lack stability. In such clashes, they have been torn asunder under the forces of persecution, dissension, desertion, and apathy.

When unions gained legal sanction in this country, workers turned to them in large numbers. In the early thirties they responded spontaneously to the proclamation that organized collective action against the employer would offer them protection against wage-cuts, speed-ups, and arbitrary exercise of unrestrained power by management and an opportunity for improving their lot. Out of this confidence that trade unionism was an answer to their frustrations and a means for satisfying their longings, the current movement was born. Their successes assured their growth.

No formal description exists of the new personality profile of the organized worker, but it is vastly different from that of the early thirties. In in-plant attitudes, the present American worker is more disciplined; he looks not to intermittent eruptions but to systematic pursuit of his grievances and regular review of contract terms for correction of irritations and attainment of new gains. Self-respect and rationality pervade the relations between worker, union official and company administrators and negotiators. The narrowing of the economic and social gaps among manual workers, supervision, and white-collar workers has reinforced the worker's self-confidence and esteem. Within the community, the higher income and availability of alternative jobs have produced a new respect for workers. The manual worker is looking more to voluntary joint action with other citizens than to his class groups for an effective voice in community affairs.[2]

[2] The existence of millions of unorganized workers does not negate the above conclusions. Repression, coercion, and the diminution, if not the almost complete elimination, of legal protection have stalled union growth in many areas. In more isolated areas, particularly in the South, workers are insulated from contact with unions and have no clear image of their value. Their aloofness has also been reinforced by anti-union propaganda. The numbers of the organized have not risen as much as the union movement desired because many workers

TECHNIQUES FOR EFFECTING GAINS

At the shop work unit level, the adequacy of union activities can be readily tested. Grievance machinery has been adopted widely. To an increasing degree complaints are being handled maturely. Professional industrial relations people are aware of the value of satisfactory handling of grievances, and their staffs tend to be adequate for this purpose. Union shop stewards, committees, and business agents have developed real expertness in processing complaints by helping the worker determine, formulate, and pursue them through appropriate channels. In no area of industrial relations have unions, management, colleges, and government worked more persistently than in the training of participants in the grievance process and preparation of material for improving its effectiveness. Results have been highly satisfactory. Widespread acceptance of arbitration of grievances has also accelerated the adoption of more thorough and liberal systems of grievance handling.

Where the formal grievance process does not function because of resistances within union administrative structures, workers usually can apply effective pressure through shop cliques. Under the protection of the union, these informal groups can be readily constituted and do, in fact, multiply in plants. In many places they are indispensable to the formal union machinery. Through impressive presentations, numbers, persistence, or political threats, they are able to pressure leaders on specific issues as well as to exercise influence on or substitute for the locals on matters over which the union itself is not prone to act. And in the last analysis, they can turn to open political forums, membership meetings, and, finally, elections of officers to pursue and gain acceptance of their position within the union. Making full use of these alternatives remains the most challenging problem of political democracy within unions. But on the other hand, these smaller groups often succeed in com-

---

have seen no immediate material advantage in joining unions. Labor shortages and high business profits have led to the adoption of union standards in non-union shops and prompted the removal of many irritating pressures. Individuals are better able to fend for themselves in this era of full employment. Non-manual workers continue to shy away from unionism despite the relative deterioration of their employment standards. They continue to cling to older myths that group action is of dubious propriety for their ranks.

mitting unions to positions which hardly affect the whole body and at times are at variance with it. Some strikes result from the union's acceptance of the cause of a special group.

For the individual, the grievance process affords a direct approach to the resolution of complaints which are usually the result of contract violations or local irritations. The satisfaction of more fundamental longings, e.g., realization of fundamental economic gains or the correction of more basic inequities, requires revisions of the collective agreement, enactment or revision of laws, or issuance of favorable decisions by public agencies.

The member may become involved both in the process of definition of goals and in determination of strategy and tactics in the actual execution of the broader program. Even with respect to the former, members rely primarily upon informal communications for voicing their views. Their occasional proposals are apt to be impulsive expressions of opinion rather than concrete or matured proposals. The great mass prefer to turn the responsibility of formulating demands over to the union leadership, which in turn is dependent not only on its sensitivities and insights but also upon formal communications from shop stewards and less formal sources of information. Beyond the shop level, the relaying of goals and proposals is more formal since conferences and meetings are frequent and the participants include both the active core of local members and the officialdom.

Not all procedures work smoothly or effectively. Local unions have often protested or rebelled against the goals set by leaders. The membership in such cases has overridden the leadership. In small plant negotiations for a single company, dissenting groups often hold up formulations until differences can be ironed out with specific concessions to the minority.

Individual participation is even more restricted in the negotiations with groups of employers, or lobbying with public agencies or appearances before public bodies. The union leadership and representatives usually shoulder the full responsibility, with the individual sharing in the experience only to the degree that details of the activity are adequately reported back to the membership. The representative relationship dominates these union activities. The inadequacy of downward union communication, except on matters directly affecting the worker, deprives many workers of the profound psychological benefits of membership.

In the implementation of programs for strategy and tactics, as well as in the process for affecting approval or disapproval of proposals or agreements, the individual has many opportunities for sharing in the experience and indeed is often compelled to participate. Union meetings on the shop, department, plant, or local union levels are numerous, and pass on problems and determine policies of consequence to the individual. Even more significant from the point of view of individual identification are economic battles such as sit-downs, slow-downs, strikes, demonstrations, and boycotts in which the individual must participate. The success of the undertaking depends upon his support. In successful experiences, pride in accomplishment increases the tie to unionism.

Individuals like to avoid a prominent part in these episodes and prefer to retire to anonymity or to passive positions, in part to escape exposure. To combat these trends, unions on occasions resort to techniques to cajole, to promote, and in the more critical economic conflicts to coerce individuals into activity. This is a force exercised by his own group, not by an economically antagonistic one. Group pressures and informal appeals from the leadership often are adequate, but in other instances various penalties are employed.

Extreme tests of loyalty occur in the case of strikes, particularly prolonged ones, when the individual must subordinate his own and his family's immediate well-being to the long term good of the group. Techniques for maintaining morale, support, and determination are widely known and effectively mastered by the trade union movement. Tensions and strains of these strifes produce personal problems which at times may endanger the entire venture. But the workers' willingness to accept these challenges is confirmed by the recurrent use of strikes and the endurance shown by workers. Outside propaganda and political pressures are generally ineffective against the striker driven by a conviction that his cause is right.

INSTITUTIONAL ACTIVITIES

The current preoccupation of trade unions with immediate economic goals has limited their other activities. In days of less effective union operation and lesser strength, the difficulties of scoring advances and the unfriendliness of employers and political groups, as well as discriminatory practices and class lines within the community and the absence of community facilities, inspired more class identity and evoked a greater need for specialized activities. Unions tended to provide a wider range of affairs and institutions to meet members' needs. Now there is less call for them from the great mass of members.

Even with respect to the ordinary and necessary procedures of formal organizations such as union meetings, committees and reports, elections, and formal activities, the vast majority of members like American citizens generally, prefer that these be carried on by the core of interested persons ("activity"), believing in part that continuous supervision is not required or at least will not provide any great advantage, and that they are only tangential to the union's major purpose of improving conditions through collective bargaining. The great body of membership intercedes only when aroused on specific issues or pressured into participation.

Nevertheless, the leadership is aware of the ever-present need for promoting loyalty and attachment to the union to assure a high priority for its values and decisions in competition with outside pressures, particularly those of the employer, and the immediate personal interests of the individual. Unions seek to implant this priority through education, through reliance upon the sheer forcefulness of or the satisfactions resulting from their routine activities and achievements, or through the workers' own orientation. Unions emphasize such attitudes as workers' rights to economic benefits and development, effectiveness of collective action, feeling of belonging to a worker group, loyalty to fellowmen, and the conviction that employer judgments and interests are not superior to the workers' own interests.[3]

[3] The achievement of this high degree of membership loyalty to the trade union must be contrasted with management's less rewarded efforts to awaken a similar feeling to the business enterprise. In part its feebler results may be ascribed to the reduction in the demands for such loyalty to the enterprise. Both management and employee are encouraged to seek better opportunities wherever they may be. Moreover, plant abandonment based on completely economic calculations is a common experience. High economic activity and the opportunities for alternative employments have minimized the need for giving high priorities to the survival of a specific establishment. The current employment code tends more nearly to emphasize enthusiastic discharge of job responsibilities than the subordination of personal interest to the enterprise.

Union educational efforts are now primarily utilitarian in character, designed to improve member performance in the operation of the union. Unions have not undertaken, except in unusual instances, to compete with community social agencies. Rather they have sought to democratize these organizations and their attitudes to insure better services. The same approach also pervades other fields such as politics and educational, recreational, and leisure-time activities. Unions have not become the center of a way of life but rather an agency for effecting a better mode of living.[4]

LEADERSHIP, PERSUASION, AND REPRESENTATION

Since the membership as individuals and as a body is concerned with satisfying its longings and obtaining economic gains and status with the aid of the union, the success of the institution itself is dependent upon its effectiveness in bringing these aspirations and desires to the surface and providing shrewd leadership for their realization. Opportunities for upward communication exist through formal and informal channels within the union's body politic. The shop steward is a key figure, for his responsibility is to represent and speak for his group. His sensitivities and discernments can help considerably in this system of upward communication.

The trade union rests upon its ability to create cohesion and effect unified action among its members and to use this force to bargain with and influence employer, community, and political groups. Its leverage is massed economic power. Its effective use is usually advanced by capable leaders. While their capacity is not always critical or indispensable to success, incompetence may frustrate and delay the formation of the union and weaken the position and bargaining power of the organized group. Extreme inadequacy in the leadership of organized groups is rare and does not continue for long, but it has been observed for protracted periods in the ranks of organizers.

The powers of persuasion and leadership can determine the degree of unity and the members' readiness to follow and pursue

[4] A number of organizations have provided other services such as cooperative housing projects, banks and credit unions, employment offices, assistance in processing applications for unemployment insurance, workmen's compensation, old age pensions, medical, sickness, or injury benefits, and death benefits. In a period when the economic drive may not be sufficient to maintain loyalties or worker identities, these services may multiply.

established policies and programs. The leadership group carries the responsibility for defining specific goals, strategy, tactics, and the course of conduct. The leaders carry on the negotiations and present proposed agreements to the membership with recommendations for action. In strikes, they constitute the strategists and leaders. In them are also vested the responsibilities for the routine operation of the union. Unions benefit or suffer from the leaders' capacities and deficiencies.

Members of the leadership group usually do not build up to a single hierarchy with well-defined relations among the constituent individuals. There is, more often than not, no formal line of responsibility, because under our systems of union organization and certification of collective bargaining agents, ultimate authority rests with the local unit. Higher groupings are combinations of locals which are, at times, broken up and rearranged. Their relations to locals are defined in union constitutions. Leaders at the higher echelons must look to local union leadership for support at elections and conventions.

Even within locals, the power seats may be widely dispersed among shop stewards, grievance committeemen, and other officials. By controlling their own following they can enhance their political position and bargaining power with other leaders, either for their own advancement or for the promotion of the group's interests. Intergroup political conflicts are not uncommon in locals.

The reality of power is reflected in the continued insistence on local union autonomy in the widest possible areas and the acceptance of this principle in the movement. In unions oriented to local markets, independence from central authorities is a continuing fact affecting the very nature and structure of the national organization, making it more of a coordinator of separate power groupings than a director of a single, unified agency. Unions dealing with industries in which national corporations predominate reserve many subjects for exclusive local determination to accommodate their procedure to the pressure for greater local activity. Union administration on the higher levels is a process of securing the consent among groups rather than prescribing single policies for all through a central office.

The growth of the size of unions has increased the influence of the higher echelons. Concurrent to the moves toward the dispersion of power is another pressure for recognition of the preeminence of the central leaders.

TYPES OF LEADERS

Contrasting trends on centralization highlight the different types of leaders. The most prevalent, particularly at the local levels, is the head of a coalition rather than the dominant single leader. In many instances union executives are really the agents of the group. This situation is typical of local unions without full-time paid officials. But even at higher levels, officials may seek to avoid responsibilities or may feel too insecure to offer direction. The consequence may be more than the usual amount of factionalism, indecision, and dispersion of effort. By contrast, some leaders of coalitions initiate and support consistently formulated programs and policies. They are the innovators and trail blazers, who lead with courage and imagination.

Both types of coalition leaders are responsible for keeping the balance of forces expressing themselves in differing conceptions of policy, strategy, and tactics. They act as political middlemen representing the power groups before the full membership, the employer, and the public. Interaction of power groups may promote political clashes among leaders as coalitions weaken, and personal differences encourage outright contests for power. On the other hand, more outright consultation and frequent appeals and contacts with the membership are common in these situations.

The third type is the single leader in whom power and decision-making tends to be concentrated. His number has grown with the expansion of powers and numbers within the trade unions and the long tenure of officers. While this type of leader is found most frequently at the national level, some local unions have such centralized leadership. It is most common in unions and areas where work units are small and dispersed and where specific controls exist over some phase of employment through employment offices, shape-ups on the dock, benefit payments, closed shops, or other techniques. Long tenures for officers and protracted periods of successful collective bargaining have encouraged the building up of formal political support for these leaders. Their influence is so pervasive that they actually shape the union's profile by their policies, the activities they advance, and the subordinate leadership they favor and promote. The immediate subordinates in such situations are couriers rather than independent officers.[5]

CHARACTERISTICS OF LEADERS

The type of leadership that develops at all union levels depends upon the range of responsibility, circumstances, union traditions, and local framework. In assessing leaders as personalities, several characteristics stand out. They are recruited primarily from among the people they represent. More often than not they are men. Women officers are found for the most part only at the shop steward and local committee levels. It is unusual for officials to be secured from other industries or professional personnel.

Leaders reflect the predominant value systems among members. Even the innovators among them share this common characteristic. In recent years, fewer and fewer have been dedicated to any specific ideologies or political systems. Preoccupied with the economic and political issues of collective bargaining, they are less conversant with trends in political radicalism.

The leaders' temperaments, casts of mind, and manners of speech will vary with the stage in the union's development. There are the aggressive, oratorically-bent, and uncompromising organizers, dedicated to awakening interest in unions, inciting restlessness among workers and antagonism to employers, and inspiring workers to submerge their fears and support their longings for greater rights. On the other end of the range are the dexterous, experienced union officers, skilled in the arts of negotiation of agreements and grievances, adjusted to the processes of accommodating the interests of workers and management, and able to administer the union for growth and stability. In the vast majority of cases, of course, the

[5] A distinction may be drawn between those leaders who gained power through the force of personality, personal strength, and capacity and those who reached this position with the aid of outside pressure groups and tactics. The latter type is small in number and associated with areas where racketeering has gained a foothold. The former governs through prestige and respect as well as the political organization he has forged. The latter prevails because of the fears he inspires and the political domination he has gained. While both maintain highly centralized organizations, the former will allow for a high degree of freedom of communication, consultation, and rapport with the membership, and the latter will rely primarily upon his power to guide and administer.

leaders combine these attributes, the degree depending on the personality and situation. With the growth of unions, the latter type has multiplied impressively.

Union leaders are not tutored for their assignments. They gain their skills for the wide range of problems they handle through actual encounter with them, oral communication with other leaders, members, and employers, and personal discernment. They assume their responsibilities for making judgments and decisions and direct and guide their following as soon as they are elected. Their primary resource must thereafter be their own experience and capacity rather than specific preparation for the tasks at hand. As a result, their inclinations and views are more reflective of their following than of a single system of indoctrination or education.

In their position they are the managers of the forces of discontent. Their responsibility is to direct, restrain, and unloose the economic power to the best long-term advantage of the people they lead. In the organizing stage, they build the power of concerted economic force. After there is cohesiveness in a union, it is employed to gain the people's and the union's objectives. With the goals clearly in mind, the leaders must continue to hold their following and direct its participation in and support of the union's programs. In negotiations with employers, they direct the latent economic powers of the organization into various channels. The employer must be impressed with its might. On occasions, the employees' restlessness, determination, and readiness for battle must be made evident to the employer.

Above and beyond displays of power, negotiations require adequate presentation of logical and factual material and effective argument. These exchanges can help crystallize the rationality of the terms economic power is supporting and thereby ease their acceptance and facilitate the accommodation process for the parties.

In his negotiations and general conduct the union leader relies upon the sharpness of his insights and the resourcefulness of his mind. Inventiveness and improvisation are his primary powers in working out new solutions.

The trade union leader must be flexible in temperament. He may run the gamut from conciliation to obstinate arrogance. He may be the aggressive organizer or the labor statesman or some combination of both. The inflexible man presenting the same image both within and outside the union is generally less competent in dealing with the issues and people he meets.

His outlook will be oriented toward the whole labor market rather than the individual plant or company with which he is negotiating. His approaches and views are, therefore, likely to be different from the emphasis on individual plant advantages which the employer stresses.

There are contrasting types of idealistic and job-oriented leaders. The former is moved by his drive to fight for economic rights and social justice for the worker. Disciplined by the routines of union operation, he remains a dedicated man inspiring his following to the long-term objectives.

Other men see their jobs as interesting opportunities with many personal rewards. They bring to their assignment not broad objectives but limited concepts of responsibility. They will be most routine in their conduct and move along with the membership. But the vitality behind the workers' expectations is sufficient to move these men to the fullest utilization of their personal capacities, to higher levels of leadership, and to the fulfillment of union objectives as they may be envisaged.

The trade union movement constantly finds its own leadership no matter how much management endeavors to woo its competent men. Human groups seldom lack people who become leaders even if the group itself has to alter its behavior in adjusting to the different personalities. Unions have and will continue to serve as ladders of personal success for tens of thousands of persons who would otherwise be submerged in our society. They become an outlet for the exercise of creative leadership by workers within their own field of experience.

INFLUENCES IN POLICIES AND PROGRAMS

Trade union leaders must fire their members with motive and conviction. In the organizing stage, they overcome opposition of social pressures by their powers of persuasion and elaboration of the benefits of unionism, and help sublimate personal fears and anxieties and arouse venturesomeness and bold feelings. After this spirit has been awakened and channeled into a permanent union, the longings for economic advancement and new rights appear to be self-generating in our economic environment. The release of aspirations which comes with union membership is symbolized by the noticeable increase in emphasis on wage increases among union leaders in contrast to the apparent apathy among the unorganized.

Union leaders help crystallize and give concrete form to these demands. The actual drive for improvements is deeply rooted in the members' own insistence on progress and recognition of the union as their tool for achieving these gains.

The more persuasive leaders guide the union membership in its formulations of views, policies, and specific demands. But in the United States, with its particular distaste for doctrine and theoretical discourse and the stress upon the pragmatic, the goals and ideology have been informally and progressively shaped by internal and external pressures rather than by formal policy or specific personalities. Gompers' view on nonpartisan policies, Lewis' and Hillman's espousal of industrial unionism and political action, and Reuther's formulations of economic goals have been largely products of the times rather than personal inventions and philosophies. Their influences have been pervasive, but they expressed rather than invented a position. Their intense convictions, effective and in some cases dramatic personalities, helped communicate and win support for the positions they espoused.

In appraising the union leaders' part in the development of an organizational ideology, one must be aware that, while their personal development may have been critical in bringing them into the movement, this factor is not likely to alter the stream of the movement. The stage of union development and the recency of the union's formation are the most pertinent of the outside forces. Unions in the throes of organization are likely to be oriented to militant outlooks, with aggressive leaders holding views openly critical of the current political and economic society. Internal political conflict also will condition the union's and leadership's views and policies.

Unions which have achieved substantial, mature, and successful collective bargaining relations are apt to be more moderate and optimistic in their outlook. Leaders who have gained their position through routine election rather than the arduous battles of initial union organization and the trials of organizational survival will also reflect a more stable approach to the problems of the union.

Moods of the membership and its tradition will also considerably affect a union's temper. Leaders will always reveal them in their attitudes and policies. Thus, unions among the miners, auto workers, textile and needle trades workers mirror the differences in constituencies arising out of diverse age, sex, skill, period of industrial employment, ethnic and religious characteristics, and cultural settings. The ideology and outlook will also be conditioned by the recency of organization, for early traditions are hard to shake off, even though they be obsolete.

Leaders must also take account of the views of their associates. The strong-willed and authoritarian type of executive may dominate and use the members of the executive board, the associate officers, and the unofficial leaders primarily to communicate with the members and for administering the union, but he cannot overlook their reactions. Less domineering leaders are usually responsive to colleagues' views. Local leaders and groups will not neglect the positions and views of regional and national bodies and persons. Nor will the national bodies and leaders be indifferent either to the attitudes of constituent groups or the national federations. While many mavericks and dissenters will be found, the pressure for conformance to prevailing views and policies has been particularly strong during the last twenty years. To an increasing degree, professional and specialized staffs bring ideas and materials for the development of policy and specific programs.

The responsive character of the union leaders is also affected by management and the public. Employers profoundly affect the leaders both by the type of opposition they offer and by the bargaining position they present. Whether they be controversies of words or economic power, the union leaders must match them. Employers who have turned to extended economic discussions and public debates, often in response to an earlier union effort in this direction, have forced union leaders to follow suit. Where employers prefer settlements to flow from personal deals, union leaders in many cases will respond. However, some unionists seriously dislike this procedure and reject it as part of the negotiations process. Direct personal negotiations between individual representatives of both sides are nevertheless very common.

The public itself or special groups within the community also significantly shape what union leaders do and say. During the last twenty years, the philosophy and programs of the New and Fair Deals have had profound effects on American unionism. They have, in fact, prescribed a good part of its practical program. Obligations to the Roosevelt and Truman administrations have weighed seriously the movement's public and private statements. Personal friendships between trade unionists and political officers have shaped behavior as well as policies.

Increased acceptance of private enterprise economy by the country as a whole has won over the great body of trade unionists to an endorsement of this form of economic organization. Continued existence of a high employment economy has radically changed the emphasis in speeches, moods, and programs. Public revulsion following the disclosures of abuses of union welfare funds accelerated internal investigations, remedial actions, and promulgation of codes for trustees of such funds.

STRATEGY AND TACTICS FOR UNION ACTIVITIES

Union leaders are most consequential in the determination of specific strategy and tactics for collective bargaining or legislative campaigns. As in other contests, leaders can be most critical in affecting its course as the rapidity with which issues arise requires quick and frequent decisions. Not only do they help lay out the programs but they take the pulse of the negotiations, campaign, or economic contest and suggest or arrange for changes of pace as circumstances demand. The program must be accepted and supported by the membership, but in the practical developments the leaders' influence can be most preeminent.[6]

In all struggles close contact must be maintained with the membership. The reactions, expectations, and dissatisfactions of the members must be known, and the leader in turn must communicate with his following. We have already noted the challenge and problems in upward communication.

The downward course is equally difficult to follow. Workers do

[6] Unlike the leaders of other battles, the purpose of labor conflict on the part of the union is not the destruction of the employer, but his conversion. These contests cause substantial losses to both parties, so the objectives must be to convince management of the futility of the battle and the profit of accommodation and compromise.

not readily accept generalized messages. They prefer to receive them from a familiar source, such as the shop steward or work associate. The oral is more effective than the written word. Messages couched in expressions related to their own experience are best understood. Actually, many channels must be employed to get the message across, particularly if it deals with general and not personal matters.

The gap between leadership and membership has grown with the maturity of the trade union. While the leaders are usually confident in their perception, they are beginning to recognize their limitations. In part, it is evidenced by their greater willngness to look for help from opinion polls. While union leaders are best able to sense general job dissatisfactions and demands, they underestimate the volume and specific nature thereof. They assume that workers react as they do. The larger and more diversified the bargaining unit, the more difficult it is to perceive expectations or reactions. The discernment of worker attitudes is most complicated on non-job issues. The leader who does not communicate and indoctrinate continuously tends to be the least able to keep abreast of his people. But the urgency of overcoming deficiencies in the system of communication has been recently relaxed by the successes experienced in actual negotiations. What price the movement will pay is suggested by its inability to corral trade unionists in support of announced political and legislative positions.

Union leaders continue to avoid the use of professional help except as such assistance is inescapable, as in the case of lawyers, certified public accountants, doctors, insurance men, or economists for formal economic presentations.

POLITICAL LEADERSHIP

The position of union leadership is an increasingly prized one within the trade union fraternity. The leaders make many personal sacrifices, such as irregular hours, strain, and separation from family. But the compensations in the form of satisfactions, achievements, psychic rewards, prestige, and social position are impressive. To an increasing degree financial rewards are becoming adequate. Some individuals are, in fact, handsomely paid.

Union officers tend to desire to stay in their positions. Like any political personality, to maintain himself in office in this country the official must develop a following among the membership and a political organization with appropriate subordinate leadership to support and be loyal to him. He must devote much time and energy to insure continued approval of his position by the membership. He directs programs, demands, and activities to this end. He may use newspapers and other publicity channels for spreading rewards, punishments, and patronage. Because public prestige is so helpful, many union leaders have enhanced their positions by securing outside recognition in public and governmental affairs and within the trade union movement.

Within the organization itself, the leader will employ the privileges of his position to entrench himself. He may endorse his own supporters for elective jobs or appoint them to key positions. He may assign key people in his own group to policy posts or other representative jobs. On occasion he may use his disciplinary or judicial power or appeals for unity in the ranks to reinforce his own power or position.

To ward off competition, he may encourage rivalry among the leaders of the lower echelons. Some officers conciliate their opposition, while others treat them harshly and capitalize on their own power to nullify or even suppress the influence of others. Control of the organization has also been used to prevent minorities from expressing their views and influencing union conduct. Elections have, in some cases, been rigged by incumbents to ensure their continuance in office. Abuses of power continue to be an ever-present concern for trade unionists who want to insure observance both of the form and the process of democracy within the union movement.

With the adoption of the no-raid pacts and the establishment of jurisdictional arbitration machinery, the threat of union raids has been reduced, but the challenge of secession continues. Dissenters, fighting with political tools, at times look to secession as the alternative, but it is a difficult and costly procedure to follow to gain recognition and rights for minorities.[7]

[7] One of the most mature forms of democratic union administration is provided by the party system in which leadership is maintained but is held responsible to an organized group and in which repeated contests occur among the parties for office. The regular political contest assures a constant check on the policies of the governing groups. Formal party organization is exemplified

OUTSIDE REPRESENTATION

The leader's responsibility is not only to win the support of the membership and negotiate successfully with the employer, but in an increasing number of cases to win recognition for and representation by the union in governmental and community affairs. Many union leaders promote contacts and the acceptance of unions in civic affairs. These activities have proved useful to the unions, assuring wider understanding of their activities and purposes. Many civic institutions have thereby become more accessible to workers. Their attitudes and procedures have been democratized as a result of the respect the trade unions and their representatives have gained. Good press relations as well as the acceptance by political parties assure more sympathetic attitudes toward unions and union members and are helpful in periods of conflict.

THE ADMINISTRATIVE OFFICER

One additional responsibility shouldered by the union officer is that of administering routine affairs, including the personnel issues, which are often disconcerting to the elected officer.

His normal relations within the union are with other officers and active volunteer members. In the earlier, less prosperous period, the office and professional staff shared the modest wages and long hours of union officialdom. As the staffs grew in size and the union's financial position improved, the rewards of the officials advanced and a lag developed for the staff.[8]

The union leader has a major responsibility for securing adoption of an adequate level of dues and a satisfactory system of collection.

---

by the International Typographical Union and the Newspaper Guild, but they are the exceptions rather than the rule among trade unions.

[8] The trade union movement has developed no clear philosophy or approach to the determination of wage levels for its officers and staffs. Shall they be related to the earnings of its members or shall prevailing wage standards be followed? The wide dispersion of the salaries of union presidents of comparable size and resources epitomizes this confusion. The gap is even more striking in the wage levels for the staffs. Increasingly, the trend has been toward accepting community standards, but it has been achieved with hesitance and confusion. But they are being held to accounting by their own commitments to union organization, collective bargaining, and decent rewards. There is, therefore, an increased tendency to recognize the nonpolitical staff as employees and accept formal systems of collective bargaining.

With increased acceptance of the checkoff system, this problem has been considerably minimized. However, the leader still shoulders the burden of securing acceptance of higher dues and other contributions when the issue arises. He must also assure proper use of funds and the balance of expenditures with income as well as the accumulation of funds for such emergencies as strikes, organizing efforts, and other contributions.[9]

THE LEADER'S TRUST

Use of authoritarian administrative procedures is a violation of trade union spirit, but capitalization of the office for personal advantage is an abuse of trust. However, this distinction is seldom drawn. Members are usually not sensitive to abuses until the opposition, maladministration or absence of progress in collective bargaining, or an outside group focuses attention on these activities.[10]

A more critical example of abuse is the use of the office for personal advantage, particularly in the form of monetary benefits or emoluments, irrespective of whether they represent an injury to the members. In the extreme forms the situation is clearly discernible. Racketeers have gained control of some unions or leaders and exploited their power to shake down employers and others. Some racketeers have combined their control of the union with management of a trade association, thereby insuring an iron grip on an industry. In other instances political machines have used unions or leaders for their purposes. Such leaders have at times neglected the members' interests, but in other cases have pressed them most conscientiously and have secured handsome benefits. The history of the

[9] The union leader also is called on to perform other services, such as acting as personal confidant and counselor to members. He is expected to offer his ear and counsel to members who believe their cause has not been adequately dealt with by the ordinary union process. He must reconcile individuals to the policies pursued by the union.

[10] A more usual charge against a leader is betrayal of the workers' interests. These occasions have been rare in recent years with such continued success in collective bargaining. The charges are more often than not the by-products of internal political conflict and reflect differences in judgment concerning the possibilities of getting better terms or the adequacy of the agreements in question. "Sellouts," i.e., betrayals of the workers' interests for the personal gain of the leader, have occurred and are likely to repeat themselves in such a highly decentralized institution with so many seats of local power and with the prevalence of closed negotiations between the principal negotiators. But they are exceptional.

trade union movement contains many brilliant episodes of international unions fighting racketeer groups, but there are also sordid chapters of indifference toward this misuse of unions by predatory groups.[11]

UNION MEMBERS' REACTION

During the last two decades trade unions have rolled up a record of unparalleled achievements. The membership has responded with steadfast loyalty. While they may have appeared casual in their attitudes, on matters central to the union's function they have recurrently displayed a determination and spirit which reflect their identification with the union. The response to strike calls and other moments of trial is confirmation of the deep hold which the unions have on their members.

A vast number of members participate in regular union activities. It is estimated that one out of twenty holds some type of office. These are the people who have positive and articulate attitudes, and they are missionaries for the cause of unionism. But, with a few dramatic exceptions, the majority relies upon the leaders to formulate and present programs and practices to them. Rebellions in labor's ranks have in recent years been few and far between.

Despite this strong attachment, many unionists remain ill-informed about and unable to express the movement's views, beliefs, expectations, and programs. Efforts at indoctrination have been limited in recent years. The more removed an issue is from the job, the less knowing are members concerning it. The less active the member, the less informed he is of the union's views and the less sensitive he is to its value system. In crucial tests of union influence on members on noneconomic issues where broad mass participation is necessary, the union is unable to count on carrying its following with it. The absence of an active process of indoctrination has handicapped the movement. Recognition of this shortcoming is

[11] More recently, kickbacks on group insurance policies have encouraged mismanagement and malfeasance among individual union officers. Insurance companies and brokers, tempted by high profits, have offered all types of financial inducements to gain this business. Managers of union-administered welfare funds have been seduced by the opportunity for personal riches. Fortunately, the trade union movement has reacted strongly against these practices and has prescribed a code of conduct, but its enforcement is still a challenge for the future.

growing in the top echelons of the movement, and increased interest is visible in this area of activity.

The individual worker enjoys unusual opportunities through the union and collective bargaining process to press his gripes. They are the grist of the mill of a democratic institution. They are the pressures which correct the inequities created by uniform legislation. Where the formal system of grievance review and contract negotiations does not satisfy the individual, he can pursue informal procedures. Under the protection of union organization, formal and informal groups are constituted within the shop for exchange of views and promotion of specific programs. The individual has gained new freedom within the shop and new status within the society. Both have endeared the trade union to him.

CONCLUSION

The trade union is a mass movement depending for its basic vitality upon the aspirations and pressures of its constituency. Its strength rests upon massed economic power rather than upon the special qualities of its leaders. It has been effective because this power and members' determination have often transcended the personal capacities of its leaders and officials. The latter are its agents and spokesmen rather than the source of its original inspiration and strength. Its successes have reinforced the loyalty of its members to the institution.

The student of human relations can contribute by helping the movement to be more effective and popular, with a responsive and mature leadership which is representative, persuasive, and conscious of the democratic nature of the institution and the personal trust of leadership.